I0816773

**First published in the UK 2024 by Sona Books an imprint of Danann Media Publishing Ltd.**



Proofreader: Cameron Thurlow



CAT NO: **SON0594**
ISBN: **978-1-915343-45-1**

**Made in EU.**

# Easy CROCHET Projects

# Welcome to Easy CROCHET Projects

Easy Crochet Projects is the perfect companion for crochet crafters of any skill level who are looking to discover fun and creative new patterns. Packed with all of the basic techniques to refresh your memory, this book contains all of the information you need to complete the array of patterns inside, including a colourful tea cosy, a chunky knit scarf, baby accessories, cute amigurumi projects and more!

# Contents

**10 The essentials**
Learn everything you need to know to get started on your crocheting journey

**22 The patterns**
Test your crocheting skills with some of these fun and amazing designs

# The essentials


12 Holding your hook
Holding your yarn
Make a slipknot
Chain stitch (ch)
13 Slip stich (ss/sl st)
Working the foundation chain
14 Double crochet (dc)
Treble crochet (tr)
Double treble crochet (dtr)
Half treble crochet (htr)
15 Identifying stitches
Working rows
Join a new yarn
Changing colour
16 Turning chains
Increase
Decrease
17 Starting in the round
Working in the round
18 Fastening off
Fixing mistakes
Joining
19 Yarn weights
Hook size conversion table
Tension
20 Blocking
Additional useful terms
21 Abbreviations and symbols

# The essentials

Learn the basics to get you started on your crocheting journey

## Holding your hook

### OVERHAND (KNIFE GRIP)

This technique is also known as the knife grip, as you grip the crochet hook as if you're holding a knife. Place your hand over the hook, then support the handle in your chosen palm.

### UNDERHAND (PENCIL GRIP)

For this technique, hold the hook like a pencil (hence the name pencil grip). Hold the thumb rest between your thumb and index finger and then let the handle rest on top of your hand.

## Holding your yarn

### THE LOOSE-YARN HOLD

Holding the end of the yarn in your right hand and with your left palm facing you, weave the yarn in front of your little finger, behind your ring finger, in front of your middle finger and behind your index finger.

### THE PINKY HOLD

Looping the yarn once around your little finger may help you to keep a secure grip. Follow the instructions for the loose-yarn hold, but begin by looping the yarn around your little finger clockwise.

## Make a slipknot

### MAKE A LOOP

Wrap the yarn once around two of your fingers on your left hand to form a loop, making sure to leave a tail of at least 10cm (or longer if your pattern calls for it).

### DRAW UP A LOOP

Take the loop off the hook and grip between your thumb and fingers. Insert your hook from right to left, catch the working yarn and pull through to make a loop on your hook.

### PULL TO CLOSE THE LOOP

Grip the tail and the working yarn and pull them tight to form a knot. Pull the working yarn to tighten the loop around your hook. It needs to be able to move up and down your hook so don't pull too tight.

## Chain stitch (ch)

### YARN OVER & DRAW UP LOOP

Starting with a slipknot, move your hook underneath your yarn and pull this through the loop already on your hook.

### KEEP GOING

Keep going to create a chain of the length needed in your pattern. Try not to make the stitches too tight as this will make it difficult when working subsequent rows. Keep the stitches even or you will get an uneven edge on your piece.

### Counting chains

To count the chains, identify the Vs on the side that's facing you. Each of these is one chain. The V above the slipknot is your first chain, but don't count the loop on your hook. This is the working loop and does not count as a chain. If you are creating a very long chain , it might help to mark every 10 or 20 stitches with a stitch marker.

## Slip stich (ss/sl st)

**INTO CHAIN**
Insert your hook into the second chain from the hook. Yarn over (yo). Pull your hook back through the chain. There should be two loops on your hook.

**PULL THROUGH** Avoiding the urge to yarn over, continue to pull the yarn through the second loop on the hook. You have completed the stitch and should have one loop on your hook.

### Left handed?

All the tutorials in this book can be followed by left-handed crocheters. Simply reverse the instructions and hold the picture tutorials up to a mirror to see how you should be working. So every time you see 'Right' replace it with 'Left' and every time you see 'Clockwise' replace with 'Counterclockwise' (and vice versa)

## Working the foundation chain

**FRONT OF THE CHAIN**
Looking at the front side of your chain, you will see a row of sideways Vs, each with two loops - a top loop and a bottom loop.

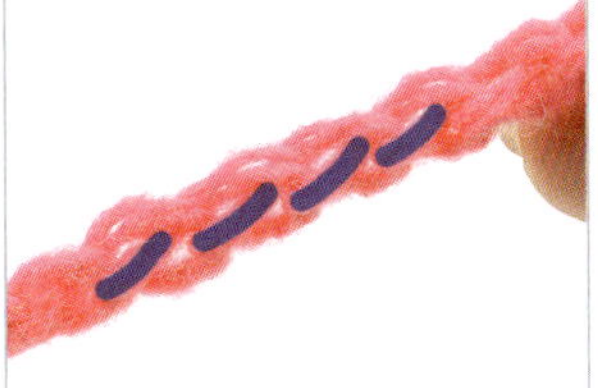

**BACK OF THE CHAIN**
When you look at the back side of the chain, you will see a line of bumps in between the loops. These are called the back bumps.

**It doesn't matter which method you use as long as you are consistent when moving along the chain. Working under the top loop is the easiest method for beginners, but does not create as neat an edge as working under the back bumps.**

1

**Method 1: TOP LOOP**
For this method, hook under the top loop only.

2

**Method 2: TOP TWO LOOPS**
Hooking under both the top loop and the back bump is sometimes referred to as the top two loops of the chain.

3

**Method 3: TOP LOOP AND BACK BUMP**
Turn over your chain so that the back bumps are facing you. Insert your hook under the back bump.

### UK and US terms

Confusingly, patterns can follow either UK or US naming conventions. To make things even more difficult, the same name is used to mean different stitches under either convention.

Most patterns will state whether they are using US or UK terminology, but if not, checking the pattern's country of origin may be a good place to start.

A handy trick to remember is that there is no stitch called a single crochet (sc) in UK terminology, so if you see this on the pattern, then you know it is using US naming conventions.

| UK | US |
|---|---|
| Chain (ch) | Chain (ch) |
| Double crochet (dc) | Single crochet (sc) |
| Treble crochet (tr) | Double crochet (dc) |
| Half treble crochet (htr) | Half double crochet (hdc) |
| Double treble crochet (dtr) | Triple (treble) crochet (tr) |
| Slip stitch (sl st/ss) | Slip stitch (sl st/ss) |

## Double crochet (dc)

**INSERT HOOK** Working into your foundation chain, find the second chain from your hook and insert your hook.

**DRAW UP A LOOP**
Yarn over (yo), then draw up a loop. You will now have two loops on your crochet hook.

**PULL TO CLOSE THE LOOP**
Yarn over and then draw the yarn through both loops on the hook so you have one loop left on your hook. You have now completed the stitch.

## Treble crochet (tr)

**INSERT HOOK** Working into your foundation chain, identify the fourth chain from your hook. Make a yarn over (yo) and then insert your hook into the fourth chain from the hook.

**YARN OVER AND DRAW UP A LOOP**
Yarn over, then draw up a loop. There should now be three loops on your hook.

**YARN OVER AND DRAW UP A LOOP**
Yarn over, then draw the yarn through two of the loops on your hook. There should now be two loops on your hook.

**COMPLETE THE STITCH**
Yarn over and then draw the yarn through the two loops left on the hook. You have completed the stitch and should have one loop on your hook.

## Double treble crochet (dtr)

**MAKE A LOOP**
Working into your foundation chain, identify the fifth chain from your hook. Yarn over twice and insert your hook into the fifth chain from the hook. Yarn over and draw up a loop. There should be four loops on your hook. Yarn over, then draw the yarn through two of the loops on your hook. There should now be three loops on your hook.

**DRAW UP A LOOP**
Yarn over, then draw the yarn through two of the loops on your hook again. There should now be two loops on your hook. Yarn over, then draw the yarn through the two loops on your hook. There should now be one loop on your hook. You have completed the stitch.

## Half treble crochet (htr)

**INSERT HOOK**
Working into your foundation chain, identify the third chain from your hook. Make a yarn over (yo) and then insert your hook into the third chain from the hook.

**YARN OVER AND DRAW UP A LOOP**
Yarn over, then draw up a loop. There should now be three loops on your hook. Yarn over, then draw the yarn through all three loops on your hook. The stitch is now complete and there should be one loop on your hook.

## Identifying stitches

There are two ways to count stitches: either by counting the Vs along the top of the work or by counting the posts. If you count the Vs, make sure you never count the loop that is on your hook. When counting either Vs or posts, you must take careful consideration when you come to the turning chain. If it is counted as a stitch in your pattern, then count it, but if not, leave it out.

## Working rows

**UNDER BOTH**
Hooking under the front and back loops of the stitch is the most common way to work into a row. Use this method unless told otherwise.

**INSERT YOUR HOOK**
After the turning chain, insert your hook so that it goes in under both the front and back loops of the V.

**FRONT AND BACK LOOPS ONLY (FLO AND BLO)**
Sometimes a pattern will say to work into Front or Back loops only. Doing so will create ridges in your work, for example, you may use FLO/BLO to add ribbing to a hat. To work into Front loops only (FLO) identify the loop closest to you and work into the stitch as normal. For Back loops, use the loop farthest away from you.

## Join a new yarn

**THE LAST STITCH**
When you think you don't have enough yarn left in your current ball, or you need to change colour, begin the last stitch of your current row with the old yarn, but stop before you reach the final step (yo and draw through all loops on hook).

**DRAW UP A LOOP**
Make a yarn over (yo) with the new ball of yarn and complete the stitch. Leave a tail of at least a 15cm (5.9in) on the new yarn. Continue crocheting with the new yarn, and drop the old yarn. You can hide the ends in the inside of your project.

## Changing colour

**ALONG THE EDGE**
When you're creating stripes by changing colour at the beginning of every row or so, you can leave the unworked yarn dangling at the edge. This way you can pick it up again when you need to. To do this, carry it loosely up the edge of the work in order to begin your new row. Adding an edge or border will hide the carried yarn strands.

**OVER THE TOP OF THE OLD YARN** If you need to change colours regularly and mid-row, crocheting over the top of the yarn you're not currently using is a good way to keep it concealed and eliminates ends that would need weaving in. This technique is great when you are creating a reversible fabric, as it keeps both sides looking neat.

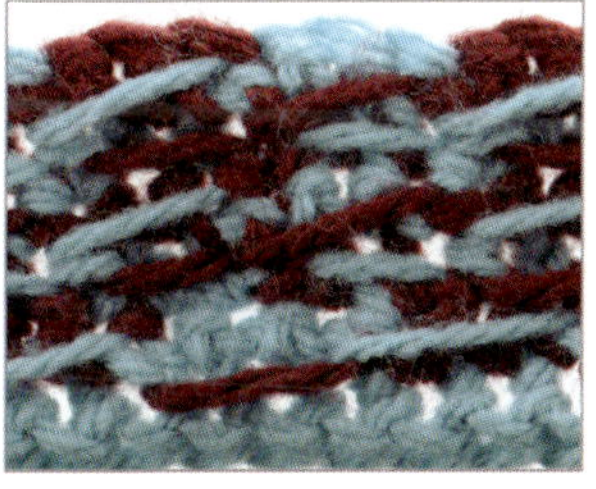

**FLOATING STRANDS**
If only one side of your final product will be seen, then you can carry the unused colours along the back of the work.Just drop the yarn you're not using, then pick it up again when you need it, loosely bringing it across the back of the work. This works best if the strands are only a few stitches long. If they are longer, cut the threads and weave in instead.

**CUTTING THE YARN**
If you are putting in a big block of one colour, it's best to cut the yarn and treat it like you're joining a new yarn, then weave in the ends of the yarn at a later stage.

## Turning chains

Whenever you turn your work, you will need to create a turning chain to start your next row. When using anything but double crochet, the turning chain always counts as the first stitch (unless specified otherwise), and the next stitch should be created in the second stitch from the hook. Different stitches need different heights of turning chains, to match the height of the stitch about to be made.

| Stitch (UK ) | Number of turning chains (t-ch) |
| --- | --- |
| Double crochet (dc) | 1 |
| Half-treble crochet (htr) | 2 |
| Treble crochet (tr) | 3 |
| Double treble crochet (dtr) | 4 |

## Increase

### INCREASING IN THE MIDDLE OF A ROW (TREBLES AS EXAMPLE)

Make a treble crochet in the next stitch. Make another treble crochet in the same stitch. You have increased your stitch count by one.

### INCREASING AT THE START OF A ROW

As the turning chain normally counts as a stitch (except in dc), increasing at the start of a row is different. To increase, insert your hook into the first stitch at the base of the chain and make the stitch. The stitch you've just made and the turning chain count as two stitches, and you have made an increase.

## Decrease

### DOUBLE CROCHET TWO STITCHES TOGETHER (DC2TOG)

Insert your hook into the next stitch, as if to make a double crochet. Draw up a loop. Without completing the stitch, insert your hook into the next stitch as if to make another double crochet. Draw up a loop. You should now have three loops on your hook. Yarn over (yo) and draw the loop through all three stitches on your hook. Having worked into two stitches, but only created one, you have decreased by one.

**TREBLE CROCHET THREE STITCHES TOGETHER (TR3TOG)** Yarn over and insert your hook into the next stitch, as if to make a treble crochet. Draw up a loop, yarn over and draw through two loops on the hook. There should now be two loops on your hook. *Without completing the stitch, yarn over and insert your hook into the next stitch. Draw up a loop, yarn over and draw through two loops on the hook.* There should now be three loops on your hook. Repeat * to * into the next stitch. There should now be four loops on your hook, yarn over and draw the yarn through all four loops to complete the decrease.

## Starting in the round

### Method 1: SINGLE CHAIN START

Chain two. Now make a double crochet (dc) into the second chain from your hook. Make the rest of your doubles into the same chain stitch as your first double crochet.

### Method 2: MULTIPLE CHAIN START

Make a short chain, depending on the pattern that you're following. Here we have shown five chains. Create a slip stitch (sl st) into the first chain that you created. Work your first round into the middle of the ring you have just made. Now either continue to work in a spiral or connect the last double crochet to the first with a slip stitch, create your turning chains and continue.

### Method 3: MAGIC RING (MR)

Also called a magic circle (mc). To begin, create a loop (as if to create a slipknot), hold the yarn where the loop crosses over, with the starting tail in front, and insert your hook from front to back.

- Yarn over with the working yarn and pull up a loop back through to the front. Yarn over your hook again, this time from above the loop, and pull through to create a chain on your ring.
- To create your first dc, insert your hook into the ring, with both the loop and starting tail above your hook. Your stitches will now be created around both yarns. Yarn over and draw up a loop back to the front of the ring. Create your stitch as you would usually. Carry on until you have the number of stitches you need.
- Once you have created all of your stitches, keep your hook in the loop and hold it and your round in your dominant hand. Pull on the starting tail to close the gap.

## Working in the round

**CONTINUOUS SPIRAL** To start each new round, work the first stitch into the top of the first stitch of the last round. Now add your stitch marker into this stitch by slipping it through the loops. Now continue to stitch the rest of your round as stated in the pattern until you reach the stitch before the marker. This is the last stitch of the round.

To start your next round, remove the marker, crochet the stitch as normal and then replace the marker into the stitch you have just created.

When finishing your spiral you will need to smooth out the jump in stitches between rows. To do so, slip stitch into the next stitch. For taller stitches, gradually crochet shorter stitches i.e if you have used tr stitches you will end with a htr, dc, ss.

**JOINED ROUNDS**

Alternatively you can add a ss at the end of each row which gives the appearance of concentric circles rather than a spiral. If you do this, to create your next round, create a chain to the height of your stitch. One for double, two for half treble, three for treble and so on.

*Turned*

*Not turned*

### Turn your work

When you create your next rows you have the choice of turning your work or continuing on around the circle (the same as a spiral stitch). Alternatively, you can turn your work at the end of each round, and it will create a slightly different look. After turning your work, you will continue to work each of the rounds the same way.

## Fastening off

### SECURE YOUR WORK

When you've finished your project, cut the working yarn about 15cm (6in) from the last stitch (or longer if your pattern states). Yarn over (yo) with the tail. Pull the yarn through the loop on your hook, and keep pulling until the cut end goes through the loop. Grab the tail and pull it tight, to close the last loop. Your stitches are now secure.

## Fixing mistakes

### UNDO YOUR WORK

When you notice that things have gone awry, take your hook out of the working loop and grab hold of the working yarn. Pull on the working yarn to unravel the stitches one by one. This process is also known as frogging. Keep pulling the working yarn until you've unravelled the mistake, then simply insert your hook into the working loop and begin redoing the work you've just undone, but this time without the mistake!

## Joining

### Method 1: WHIP STITCH

Hold two pieces together with the wrong sides facing each other. Pass your needle through the V stitches on both pieces from front to back and pull the yarn through. Draw your needle back to the front and repeat. Using a whip stitch will leave a visible line on both sides of the piece. This won't be quite as obvious when you are using the same colour.

### Method 2: MATTRESS STITCH

Lay your pieces side-by-side with the right sides facing you. Leaving a 15cm tail, insert your needle into the first edge stitch of the first piece and then down through the edge of the second. Insert your needle down through the first stitch of piece one and up through to the second stitch. Now repeat on piece two. Keep going and a loose 'ladder' will start to form. When you have done about 2.5cm, pull gently on the yarn to draw the two sides together. Repeat until you have reached the end, the seam will be almost invisible.

### Method 3: SLIP STITCH OR DOUBLE CROCHET

Insert your hook through the first stitch on both pieces. Complete a slip stitch (or double crochet) and repeat, ensuring you match up the stitches as you go.

- A slip stitch seam is strong, and will be almost invisible from the other side of the work. Slip stitches do not allow for any give, so making them too tight will pucker the fabric.
- Using a double crochet will give a more pronounced edge, giving a more decorative seam. It is also stretchier than a slip stitch join.

### Method 4: FLAT SLIP-STITCHED SEAM

Insert your hook from top to bottom through the back loop only on the right-hand piece of fabric. Do the same on your left piece, then yarn over (yo) and pull through both loops on the hook. Repeat until you reach the end. This seam produces a flat row of chain-looking stitches. It's a neat finish and adds a nice little detail to your seams.

**To join amigurumi it is helpful to pin your pieces in place. Join using one of the methods above, inserting your needle from bottom to top of the piece you are attaching. Pull tight on the yarn for a seamless join.**

## Yarn weights

| Yarn weight | Properties | Ideal for... |
|---|---|---|
| Lace, 2-ply, fingering | Extremely light, Lace yarn produces a very delicate texture on a 2mm (US 0) hook. Bigger hooks will produce a more open fabric. | Lace |
| Superfine, 3-ply, fingering, baby | Using a very slim hook, Superfine yarn is perfect for lightweight, intricate lace work. | Finely woven socks, shawls, babywear |
| Fine, 4-ply, sport, baby | Fine yarn is great for socks, and can also be used in items that feature slightly more delicate textures. | Light jumpers, babywear, socks, accessories |
| Double knit (DK), light worsted, 5/6-ply | An extremely versatile weight yarn, DK can be used to create a wide variety of items and crochets up relatively quickly. | Jumpers, light-weight scarves, blankets, toys |
| Aran, medium worsted, Afghan, 12-ply | With many yarns in this thickness using a variety of fibres to make them machine washable, Aran yarn is good for garments with thick cabled detail and functional items. | Jumpers, cabled garments, blankets, hats, scarves, mittens |
| Chunky, bulky, craft, rug, 14-ply | Quick to crochet, chunky yarn is perfect for warm outerwear. Often made from lightweight fibres to prevent drooping. | Rugs, jackets, blankets, hats, legwarmers, winter accessories |
| Super chunky, super bulky, bulky, roving, 16-ply and upwards | Commonly used with very large hooks, Super chunky yarn crochets up very quickly. Large stitches make mistakes easy to spot. | Heavy blankets, rugs, thick scarves |

## Hook size conversion table

| UK Size | US Size |
|---|---|
| 2mm, 2.25mm | B/1 |
| 2.5mm, 2.75mm | C/2 |
| 3mm, 3.25mm | D/3 |
| 3.5mm | E/4 |
| 3.75mm, 4mm | F/5 |
| 4mm, 4.25mm | G/6 |
| 4.5mm | G/7 |
| 5mm | H/8 |
| 5.5mm | I/9 |
| 6mm | J/10 |
| 6.5mm, 7mm | K/10.5 |
| 8mm | L/11 |
| 9mm | M/13 |
| 10mm | N,P/15 |

## Which hook?

Every ball of yarn comes with a recommended hook size, which is printed on the label. Use bigger hooks than this to make a more open stitch, and smaller ones to make a tighter, more compact fabric. We suggest using a smaller hook than recommended for amigurumi projects.

## Tension

Tension or gauge is the measure of how many stitches and rows you need to create a specific length and width of crocheted fabric. The size of your hook, weight of your yarn and your own tension while crocheting will all have an effect on any piece that you're creating. If you naturally crochet very tight or loose stitches, then the final product dimensions will be different to those provided in a pattern. Tension square patterns will sometimes be given with your pattern and allow you to work out how tight to make your stitches before you start. Usually these will be 10cm square.

When making things like children's toys or blankets, there is a bit more freedom when following a pattern. However, when creating garments to exact fitted measurements, tension squares are incredibly important.

With amigurumi a loose tension will show the stuffing between the stitches. It's difficult to be too tight with amigurumi, however you should still be able to work stitches reasonably easily. If needed, switch to a smaller hook for a neater finish.

*Amigurumi Tension too loose*

*Amigurumi correct tension*

## Blocking

Blocking is a process you will use after making many of your flat projects. It sets the stitches in place, adds definition to lace pieces and strengthens any straight edges in your work.

### PIN YOUR WORK

No matter which method you choose to use, you will need to pin the corners to the correct measurement for your final piece.

Next pin half way along the edge, and keep doing this until you are happy that the edges are all straight and even. If you are blocking any crocheted segments that are due to be joined, make sure you measure them out so they match when you come to sew them together.

For more refined edging, thread a blocking wire through each of the stitches or row ends along the straight edge of your project.

### Method 1: SPRAY BLOCKING

Spray blocking is the easiest and quickest way of blocking your work. Pin and then take a spray bottle and give a few sprays of water until the surface of your work is evenly saturated. Gently pat the surface to help the water absorb into the yarn fibres. Leave your work to dry; this can sometimes take over 24 hours.

### Method 2: STEAM BLOCKING

This method requires an iron or handheld steamer. Do not touch the iron to the yarn at any point. Man-made fibres will melt, and all your work and your iron will be damaged. Pin your work then hold an iron about 2.5cm (1in) from the surface of your project. Steam until the entire surface area is moist to the touch. Once done, pat the surface gently with your hands and leave to dry.

### Method 3: WET BLOCKING (BEST FOR LACE WORK)

Fill your sink or bath with lukewarm water. You can add in no-rinse wool wash if you wish. Immerse your project in the water, until saturated. Leave it for 20 minutes then take your project out and gently squeeze out the excess liquid. Do not wring your project, as this will stretch it out of shape. Continue until you can remove no more water. Lay a towel on a flat surface and lie your garment flat. Gently roll up your towel to press out even more water. Pin your project to your blocking surface (a foam mat or mattress is ideal) and leave to dry. If working on a straight-edged lace garment you will need to use a lot of pins and/or blocking wire along the edge of to obtain a professional result. The edge will bow if you don't use enough pins and spoil the finish.

## Additional useful terms

### ASTERISK* /BRACKETS( )

A symbol used to mark a point in a pattern row, usually at the beginning of a set of repeated instructions.

### CHART/STITCH DIAGRAM

A visual depiction of a crochet pattern that uses symbols to represent stitches.

### CROSSED STITCHES

Two or more tall stitches that are crossed, one in front of the other, to create an X shape.

### FIBERFILL

Toy stuffing used to stuff amigurumi projects.

### LINKED STITCH

A variation of any standard tall stitch that links the stitch to its neighbour partway up the post to eliminate the gaps between stitches and form a solid fabric.

### POST

The vertical stem of a stitch.

### POST STITCH

A stitch formed by crocheting around the post of the stitch in the row or round below, so the stitch sits in front of (or behind) the surface of the fabric.

### RIGHT SIDE (RS)

The side of a crocheted piece that's visible when finished.

### ROUND (RND)

A line of stitches worked around a circular crocheted piece.

### ROW

A line of stitches worked across a flat crocheted piece.

### SPACE (SP)

A gap formed between or beneath stitches, often seen in lace patterns.

### STITCH MARKER

A small tool you can slide into a crochet stitch to mark a position. You can use a scrap of yarn or a hairgrip instead.

### TAIL

A short length of unworked yarn left at the start or end of a piece.

### V

The two loops at the top of each stitch that from a sideways V shape; standard crochet stitches are worked into both these loops.

### WEAVE IN

A method used to secure and hide the yarn tails by stitching them through your crocheted stitches.

### WORKING LOOP

The single loop that remains on your hook after completing a crochet stitch.

### WRONG SIDE (WS)

The side of a crocheted piece that will be hidden; the inside or back.

### YARN WEIGHT

The thickness of the yarn (not the weight of a ball of yarn).

## Abbreviations and symbols

| UK stitch name | Abbreviation | Symbol | Description |
|---|---|---|---|
| back loop | BL | | The loop furthest from you at the top of the stitch. |
| back post double crochet | BPdc | | Yarn over, insert the hook from the back to the front, then to the back around the post of the next stitch, yarn over and draw up a loop, (yarn over and draw through two loops) twice. |
| chain(s) | ch(s) | | Yarn over and draw through the loop on the hook. |
| chain space(s) | ch-sp(s) | | The space beneath one or more chains. |
| double crochet | dc | or | Insert the hook into the next stitch and draw up a loop, yarn over and draw through both loops on the hook. |
| double crochet 2 together | dc2tog | | (Insert the hook into the next stitch and draw up a loop) twice, yarn over and draw through all three loops on the hook. |
| double treble crochet | dtr | | Yarn over twice, insert the hook into the next stitch and draw up a loop, (yarn over and draw through two loops on the hook) three times. |
| front loop | FL | | The loop closest to you at the top of the stitch. |
| front post treble crochet | FPtr | | Yarn over, insert the hook from the front to the back to the front around the post of the next stitch, yarn over and draw up a loop, (yarn over and draw through two loops) twice. |
| half treble crochet | htr | | Yarn over, insert the hook into the next stitch and draw up a loop, yarn over and draw through all three loops on the hook. |
| repeat | rep | | Replicate a series of given instructions. |
| skip | sk | | Pass over a stitch or stitches – do not work into it. |
| slip stitch | ss/sl st | or | Insert the hook into the next stitch, draw up a loop through the stitch and the loop on the hook. |
| stitch(es) | st(s) | | A group of one or more loops of yarn pulled through each other in a specified order until only 1 remains on the hook. |
| treble crochet | tr | | Yarn over, insert the hook into the next stitch and draw up a loop, (yarn over and draw through two loops on the hook) twice. |
| treble crochet 2 together | tr2tog | | Yarn over, insert the hook into the next stitch and draw up a loop, (yarn over and draw through two loops on the hook. |
| turning chain | t-ch | | The chain made at the start of a row to bring your hook and yarn up to the height of the next row. |
| yarn over | yo | | Pass the yarn over the hook so the yarn is caught in the throat of the hook. |

**If a pattern requires stitches that are not mentioned in this essentials section, stitch instructions will be given on the pattern page.**

# The patterns

## Clothing


24 Rose corsage
26 Spring flowers brooch
28 Fingerless shell-edge mitts
30 Cosy alpaca mittens
32 Lacy shell-edged shawl
36 Jumbo rib scarf
38 Granny square flower scarf
42 Long wave neckwarmer
44 Honeycomb belle hat
46 Scallop-edged hat and cowl
48 Boho poncho
50 A cute sweater


## Homeware


52 Squares baby blanket
56 Hushabye sleeping bag
60 Textured hot water bottle cosy
62 Spike stitch placemat and coaster
64 Linked stitches pincushion
66 Traditional tea cosy
68 Embellished bunting
70 Perky peg bag
74 Aran cushion cover
78 Spiked cushion


## Amigurumi & toys


80 Teddy bear
82 Baby sloth
84 Tiny princess
86 Sleepy sheep
88 Woodland turtle
92 Kimono doll
96 Ginger the giraffe
100 Horace the monster
104 Magical unicorn
108 Flemish giant rabbit
112 Proud lion
116 Yeti & Bigfoot
120 Pearl the dolphin
124 Baby guinea pigs
128 Tiny luck elephant
130 Happy horse
132 Trio of dinosaurs

### Pattern notes

• All our patterns are written in UK crochet terms. You can find a UK/US conversion chart on page 19.

• Each pattern comes with a star rating, which shows its difficulty. Although some are harder than others, all the stitches required can be found either in essential skills (page 12-21) or on the pattern page itself, so don't be afraid to challenge yourself!

# Rose corsage

This two-tone flower is the perfect adornment for a blouse or winter coat. Why not work up a few in different shades to co-ordinate with all your outfits?

## Difficulty

★★☆☆☆

## What you need

- 5mm hook (US H/8)
- Yarn needle
- Brooch back or safety pin
- You will need to use Aran weight yarn in your chosen colours. We have used Rowan Kid Classic in:
  Colour 1: Victoria, 852 oddments
  Colour 2: Lavender Ice, 841 oddments
  Colour 3: Spruce, 853 oddments

## Measurements

The rose measures approximately 8cm (3¼in) across, excluding leaves.

## Special stitches

Triple treble crochet (ttr): Yarn over 3 times, insert hook in stitch, yarn over and pull up loop *yarn over and draw through 2 loops* 4 times.

Quadruple treble crochet (qtr): Yarn over 4 times, insert hook in stitch, yarn over and pull up loop *yarn over and draw through 2 loops* 5 times.

## Pattern

### Rose

With 5mm hook and Colour 1, make 35 ch.

Row 1: 1 tr in 5th ch from hook (counts as 1 tr, 1 ch, 1 tr), *1 ch, miss 1 ch, (1 tr, 1 ch, 1 tr) all into next ch (making a 'V' stitch); rep from * to end (16 'V' sts.) Turn.

Row 2: Make 3 ch (counts as 1 tr), 5 tr in 1st ch sp, *1 dc in next ch sp, 6 tr into next ch sp (one shell stitch made); rep from * to end, fasten off colour 1, turn.

Row 3: Join in Colour 2 and make 1 ch, 1 dc in every st to end.

Fasten off.

### Leaf (Make 2)

With 5mm hook and Colour 3, make 11 ch.

Rnd 1: 1 htr into 3rd ch from hook, 1 tr in next ch, 1 dtr in next ch, 1 ttr in next ch, 1 qtr in next ch, 1 ttr in next ch, 1 dtr in next ch, 1 tr in next ch, (htr, 3 dc, htr) all in last ch, turn and continue working across the lower chain edge, thus: 1 tr in next ch, 1 dtr in next ch, 1 ttr in next ch, 1 qtr in next ch, 1 ttr in next ch, 1 dtr in next ch, 1 dtr in next ch, 1 tr in next ch, then (1 htr, 2 dc) into 1st ch, ss to htr from beginning of round to join.

Fasten off.

### Finishing

Darn in all ends. Coil the flower strip up and stitch together across back to hold in place. Stitch leaves to the reverse of the rose.

Sew on safety pin or brooch back, as desired.

Designed by
**Donna Jones**

Donna designs, edits and teaches yarn crafts. She believes creative expression is essential for our well-being and aims to instil this in others. Follow her on Instagram @djonesdesigns
www.donnajonesdesigns.co.uk

### Pattern notes

- If your rose seems larger/smaller than stated, try with a slightly smaller/larger hook. You can easily change the scale of the corsage by using a different size of hook with finer/thicker yarn, or several yarns held together for interesting effects.
- The rose with or without leaves can also be attached to a hair clip, barrette or hair band for a pretty accessory to dress up or down.

# Spring flowers brooch

Create this beautiful, and simple, spring brooch in whatever colours you like to add a flourish of colour to any outfit

## Difficulty

★★☆☆☆

## What you need

- 4mm hook (US G/6)
- Yarn needle
- Brooch back or safety pin
- Sewing needle and thread
- You will need to use Aran weight yarn in your chosen colours. We have used DMC Woolly yarn in:
  Colour 1: Orange Shade 10 (oddment)
  Colour 2: Cream Shade 03 (oddment)
  Colour 3: Lime Green Shade 81 (oddment)

## Measurements

Each flower measures 9cm across.

## Pattern

### Flower

With 4mm hook and col 1, make a magic ring.

Rnd 1: ch 2 (not counted as a st), 16 htr into magic ring, skip the beginning ch 2 and sl st into first htr to join (16 sts).
Pull the magic ring closed.

Rnd 2: *ch 2, skip next st, sl st in next st; rep from * another 7 times, working the last sl st into the base of the first ch 2 (8 sl st and 8 ch 2 spaces.)

Rnd 3: (1 dc, 1 tr, 2 dtr, 1 tr, 1 dc) all into each ch 2 space (beneath the 8 sl st) around, sl st into first dc to join (8 petals).

Rnd 4: *ch 4, 1 dc in the space between the next 2 petals, then lift the chain over the petal so that it sits behind it; rep from * around, sl st into the base of the beginning ch 4, cut yarn and fasten off. Make sure that all of the ch 4 loops are sitting behind a petal
(8 x ch 4 loops behind petals).

Rnd 5: Join col 2 with sl st to any ch 4 loop. ch 1
(not counted as a st),
(1 dc, 1 tr, 3 dtr, 1 tr, 1 dc) all into the same ch 4 space,
(1 dc, 1 tr, 3 dtr, 1 tr, 1 dc) into each remaining ch 4 space around, sl st to beginning ch 1 (8 petals).

Rnd 6: Repeat Round 4. Cut yarn and fasten off.

Rnd 7: Join col 3 with a sl st to any ch 4 loop. ch 1
(not counted as a st),
(1 dc, 1 tr, 4 dtr, 1 tr, 1 dc) all into the same ch 4 space, (1 dc, 1 tr, 4 dtr, 1 tr, 1 dc) into each remaining ch 4 space around.
Cut yarn and fasten off. Weave all ends into wrong side of flower and trim.

### Center

With 4mm hook and col 2 or col 3, make a magic ring.

Rnd 1: ch 1 (not counted as a st), 6 dc into magic ring, sl st to first dc to join (6 sts).
sl st into next st and fasten off. Make a knot in the centre of a short length of contrast yarn and thread through the centre. Sew to the front of flower.

### Finishing

Sew a brooch back to the flower. Make as many flowers as you like using a different order of colours for each round of petals.

Designed by
**Lynne Rowe**

Lynne Rowe is a freelance knit and crochet designer, technical editor, craft author and tutor. Lynne loves to pass on her skills to help others to knit, crochet and create. Read more about Lynne's yarn adventures at:
www.thewoolnest.blogspot.co.uk and
www.knitcrochetcreate.com

# Fingerless shell-edge mitts

When it's cold, but you still want to use your fingers for crocheting, these mitts will keep your hands warm

## Difficulty

★★☆☆☆

## What you need

- 4mm hook (US G/6)
- Yarn needle
- You will need DK weight yarn in your chosen colours. We have used Rowan Pure Wool in:
  Colour 1: Enamel, 013 (50g)

## Tension

18 stitches and 10 rows = 10 x 10cm (4 x 4in) using 4mm (US G/6) hook.

## Measurements

To fit medium female hand.
Finished size: 18cm (7in) around palm, length 13cm (5in). Mitts can be adjusted to fit – see pattern notes.

## Pattern

### Mitt (make 2)

Using 4mm hook, make 22 ch.

Row 1: 1 tr in 4th ch from hook (counts as 2 tr), 1 tr into each ch to end, turn. (20 sts)

Row 2: 3 ch (counts as 1 tr), miss st at base of ch, 1 tr in each st to end, turn.

Row 3: Repeat Row 2.

Row 4 (make thumbhole): 3 ch (counts as 1 tr), miss st at base of ch, 1 tr in next 4 sts, 7 ch, skip next 7 sts, 1 tr in each st to end, turn.

Row 5: 3 ch (counts as 1 tr), miss st at base of ch, 1 tr in next 7 sts, 1 tr in each next 7 sts, 1 tr in each st to end, turn. (20 sts).

Repeat Row 2 for 11 rows.

### Edging

Turn your work 90 degrees clockwise and begin working along the row ends as follows:

Row 1: 1 ch (does not count as a st), 2 dc in each st to end, turn. (32 sts).

Row 2 (shell edge): 1 ch (does not count as a st), 1 dc in first st, *miss 2 sts, (3 tr, 1 ch, 3 tr) all in next st, miss 2 sts, 1 dc in next st* 5 times, 1 dc in next st. (5 shells worked).

Fasten off.

### Finishing

Weave in the ends and then block lightly if desired. Sew the seam using whip stitch, or mattress stitch if preferred.

### Pattern notes

- The mitts are made from a rectangle of trebles with a thumbhole and simple shell edging. They are seamed along the middle of your palm rather than at the side as this can be more comfortable when worn.
- If you would like your mitts to be longer at the cuff then simply add more stitches. You can also adjust the width by adding (or subtracting to make smaller) a row at each side of the thumbhole

Designed by
**Dany Dalley**

Dany taught herself to crochet using the 'guide' sections in pattern books like this one. Soon she began to personalise patterns by tweaking here and there. The challenge was on then to create items from scratch! Dany also enjoys helping others take those first tentative steps in crochet and knitting.

# Cosy alpaca mittens

Why not keep your hands warm with a pair of luxurious 100% alpaca mittens - perfect for the winter season!

## Difficulty

★★☆☆☆

## What you need

- 4mm hook (US G/6)
- Yarn needle
- For this project you will need DK weight 100% alpaca yarn, in your chosen colours We used The Big Scary Bear: 100% British Alpaca in:
  Colour 1: Pebble; 50g
  Colour 2: Cream; 50g

## Tension

18 htr in the round measures 10cm.

## Measurements

18cm long x 20cm around.

## Special stitches

**Front post treble crochet (FPtr):** Yarn over, insert the hook from front to back then to the front around the post of the next stitch, yarn over and draw up a loop, (yarn over and draw through two loops) twice.

**Back post treble crochet (BPtr):** Yarn over, insert the hook from back to front then to the back around the post of the next stitch, yarn over and draw up a loop, (yarn over and draw through two loops) twice.

## Pattern

### Main mitten (make 2)

Using col 1 and starting at the top of the mitten, ch 34, ss into first ch to join into a ring.

**Rnd 1 (RS):** ch 2 (not counted as a st here and throughout), 1 htr in same st at base of ch 2, 1 htr in each st around, ss into top of first htr to join, changing to col 2, turn (34 sts).

**Rnd 2:** ch 2, 1 htr in same st at base of ch 2, 1 htr in each st around, ss into top of first htr to join, turn.

**Rnd 3:** ch 2, 1 htr in same st at base of ch 2, 1 htr in each st around, ss into top of first htr to join, changing to col 1, turn. Cut col 2.

**Rnds 4-6:** Rep round 2.

**Rnd 7:** ch 2, 1 htr in same st at base of ch 2, 1 htr in each of next 16 sts, 2 htr in next st, 1 htr in each of next 16 sts around, ss into top of first htr to join, turn (35 sts).

**Rnd 8:** ch 2, 1 htr in same st at base of ch 2, 1 htr in each of next 13 sts, ch 7, skip next 7 sts, 1 htr in each of next 14 sts, ss into top of first htr to join, turn (28 htr and 7 ch).

**Rnd 9:** ch 2, 1 htr in same st at base of ch 2, 1 htr in each of next 13 sts, 1 htr in each of next 7 ch, 1 htr in each of next 14 sts, ss into top of first htr to join, turn (35 sts).

**Rnds 10-12:** Rep round 2.

**Rnd 13:** ch 2, 1 htr in same st at base of ch 2, 1 htr in each of next 16 sts, htr2tog, 1 htr in each of next 17 sts around, ss into top of first htr to join, turn (34 sts).

**Rnds 14-18:** Rep round 2.

**Rnd 19:** 3 ch (counts a 1 FPtr), 1 BPtr in next st, *1 FPtr in next st, 1 BPtr in next st; rep from * around, ss into top of beginning 3ch (do not turn).

**Rnds 20-23:** Rep Round 19, changing to Cream on ss of round 23.

**Rnds 24-25:** In col 2, rep round 19. Fasten off.

### Top edge

Rejoin col 2 to any st around top edge.

**Rnd 26:** ch 2 (not counted as st), 1 htr in each st to end, ss into top of first htr to join (34 sts). **Rnds 27-28:** Repeat Round 19 of Main Mitten.

Fasten off.

### Finishing

Weave in ends to WS and trim.

Designed by
**Lynne Rowe**

Lynne Rowe is a freelance knit and crochet designer, technical editor, craft author and tutor. Lynne loves to pass on her skills to help others to knit, crochet and create. Read more about Lynne's yarn adventures at: www.thewoolnest.blogspot.co.uk and www.knitcrochetcreate.com

## Pattern notes

- For the Main Mitten pattern, each round is joined and work is turned ready for the next round.
- The beginning ch 2 of each round is not counted as a stitch. It is used to help create an invisible join.
- When joining each round, skip the beginning ch 2 and ss to top of first htr.
- The first stitch of each round is worked in the same st at the base of the beginning ch 2.

# Lacy shell-edged shawl

When the weather turns cooler, a shawl is the perfect garment to wear on days when a coat is too much

## Difficulty

★ ★ ★ ☆ ☆

## What you need

- 5 mm hook (US H/8)
- Yarn needle
- You will need DK weight yarn in your chosen colour. We have used Mirasol Sulka Nina in:
  Colour 1: Coral, 7113 (300g)

## Tension

15 sts and 20 rows = 10 x 10cm (4 x 4in) over treble stitch using 5mm (US H/8) crochet hook, or size required to obtain correct tension

## Measurements

The finished shawl measures 160cm (63in) along the top edge and 81cm (31¾ in) deep measured from the top centre to the bottom tip of shawl, after blocking.

## Pattern

### Main section

Using 5mm hook, make a magic ring, then work 3 ch (counts as 1 tr), 2 tr, 2 ch, 3 tr into the ring, pull ring closed, turn. (6 sts – 2 groups of 3 tr)

Row 1 (inc): 3 ch (counts as 1 tr), 2 tr into tr at base of ch, 1 tr into each tr to ch sp, (2 tr, 2 ch, 2 tr) all into ch sp, 1 tr into each tr to last st, 3 tr into 3rd of 3 ch, turn. (14 sts – 2 groups of 7 tr)

Row 2 (inc): 3 ch (counts as 1 tr), 1 tr into tr at base of ch, 1 tr into each tr to ch sp, (2 tr, 2 ch, 2 tr) all into next ch sp, 1 tr into each tr to last st, 2 tr into 3rd of 3 ch, turn. (20 sts - 2 groups of 10 tr)

Repeat Row 2 for 34 rows. Each repeated row increases your stitch count by 6.

(You should have a total of 224 sts – 2 groups of 112 tr).

Do not fasten off.

### Border - leaf pattern

Commence leaf pattern, as follows:

Row 1: ch 3 (counts as 1 tr), 3 tr in st at base of ch, miss 2 tr, 1 dc in next tr, [miss 2 tr, 7 tr in next tr, miss 2 tr, 1 dc in next tr] 18 times, (2 tr, 2 ch, 2 tr) all in 2-ch sp, 1 dc in next tr, miss 2 tr, [7 tr in next tr, miss 2 tr, 1 dc in next tr, miss 2 tr] 18 times, 4 tr in 3rd of 3 ch, turn. (1 half shell, and 18 full shells on each side of the centre (2 tr, 2 ch, and 2 tr) stitches)

Row 2 (inc): Make 3 ch (counts as 1 tr), 1 tr in st at base of ch (1 st increased), 3 ch, miss 3 tr, 1 tr in next dc, [3 ch, miss 3 tr, 1 tr in next tr, 3 ch, miss 3 tr, 1 tr in next dc] to 2 tr before 2-ch sp, 2 ch, miss 2 tr (2 tr, 2 ch, 2 tr) in 2-ch sp, 2 ch, miss 2 tr, [1 tr in next dc, 3 ch, miss 3 tr, 1 tr in next tr, 3 ch, miss 3 tr] to last dc, 1 tr in next dc, 3 ch, miss 3 tr, 2 tr in 3rd of 3 ch (1 st increased), turn.

Row 3 (inc): Make 1 ch (does not count as a st), 1 dc in st at base of ch, 1 ch (1 st increased), [1 dc in next tr, 3 ch] to 2 tr before 2-ch sp, miss 2 ch and 1 tr, 1 dc in next tr, (2 dc, 2 ch, 2 dc) all in centre 2-ch sp, 1 dc in next tr, 3 ch, miss 1 tr and 2 ch, 1 dc in next tr, [3 ch, 1 dc in next tr] to last st, 1 ch, (1 st increased) 1 dc in 3rd of ch 3, turn.

Row 4 (inc): Make 3 ch (counts as 1 tr), 3 tr in st at base of ch (1 st increased), 1 dc in next dc, [7 tr in next dc, 1 dc in next dc] to 3 dc before 2-ch sp, miss 2 dc, 4 tr in next dc, (2 tr, 2 ch, 2 tr) all in centre 2-ch sp, 4 tr in next dc, miss 2 dc and 3 ch, 1 dc in next dc, [7 tr in next dc, 1 dc in next dc] to last dc, 4 tr in next dc 1 st increased), turn.

(1 half shell, 19 full shells and another half shell on each side of the centre (2 tr, 2 ch, 2 tr) stitches)

Rows 5-13: Rep Rows 2-4, 3 times.

(1 half shell, 23 full shells and another half shell on each side of the centre (2 tr, 2 ch, 2 tr) stitches)

### Commence fan edging

Row 14: ch 3 (counts as 1 tr), miss 4 tr, V st in next dc, [5 ch, miss 7 tr, V st in next dc] to 6 tr before 2-ch sp, 5 ch, miss 6 tr, (2 tr, 2 ch, 2 tr) all in 2 ch sp, 2 ch, miss 6 tr, V st in next dc, [5 ch, miss 7 tr, V st in next dc] to last 4 tr, 3 ch, ss to top of 3 turning ch from 12th row, turn.

Row 15: ch 1, 1 dc in st at base of ch, tr in 1-ch sp at centre of next V st, [working over next 5 ch on prev row so as to enclose it, work 1 dc in 4th tr of next shell from row 13, 9 tr in 1-ch sp at centre of next V st] to last 2 tr before centre 2-ch sp, 7 tr in next tr, miss 1 tr, (2 tr, 2 ch, 2 tr) all in 2-ch sp, 7 tr in next tr, miss 1 tr, work 1 dc in 1st tr of 4-tr shell from row 13, [9 tr in 1-ch sp at centre of next V st, work 1 dc in 4th tr of shell from row 13 as before] to last V st, 9 tr in 1-ch sp at centre of next V st, 1 dc in 1st of 3 ch from beg of prev row, turn.

Row 16: ch 4 and 1 tr in st at base of ch, (counts as V st), [5 ch, miss 9 tr, V st in next dc] ending in last dc before centre 2-ch sp,

Designed by
Donna Jones

Donna designs, edits and teaches yarn crafts. She believes creative expression is essential for our well-being and aims to instil this in others. Follow her on Instagram @djonesdesigns
www.donnajonesdesigns.co.uk

5 ch, miss 2 tr, (2 tr, 2 ch, 2 tr) all in 2-ch sp, 5 ch, miss 7 tr, V st in next dc, [5 ch, miss 9 tr, V st in next dc] to end.

**Row 17:** ch 3 (counts as 1 tr), 4 tr in 1-ch sp at centre of next V st, [working over next 5 ch on prev row so as to enclose it, work 1 dc in 5th tr of next shell from row 15, 9 tr in 1-ch sp at centre of next V st] to last 2 tr before centre 2-ch sp, 7 tr in next tr, miss 1 tr, (2 tr, 2 ch, 2 tr) all in 2-ch sp, 7 tr in next tr, miss 1 tr, work 1 dc in 1st tr of 4-tr shell from row 13, [9 tr in 1-ch sp at centre of next V st, work 1 dc in 4th tr of shell from row 13 as before] to last V st, 9 tr in 1-ch sp at centre of next V st, 5 tr in 1-ch sp at centre of next V st.

Fasten off.

## Finishing

Darn in ends. Gently spray block and pinning it out flat, gently ease into shape as per finished dimensions. Ensure that the top edge lies straight and the edging is pulled out slightly to emphasise the shell pattern.

## Pattern notes

- Shawl is worked from the top downwards, forming a fabric which resembles two triangles that lie each side of a central 'spine'.
- Check you have the correct number of stitches at the end of each row or half row. Spotting a mistake earlier on will save you a lot of frustration.

# Jumbo rib scarf

This is an ideal project to make if you're new to crochet as the thick yarn and large hook will mean that you'll complete it in no time

## Difficulty

★★☆☆☆

## What you need

- 12mm hook (US O/17)
- Yarn needle/bodkin
- Sharp scissors
- You will need super chunky weight yarn in your chosen colours. We have used Hayfield Super Chunky with Wool in: Colour 1: Poole; 56 (700g)

## Tension

7 stitches and 6 rows = 10 x 10cm (4 x 4in) over rib pattern using 12mm (US O/17) hook.

## Measurements

24cm (9½in) wide and 210cm (82¾in) long, excluding fringe.

## Special stitches

Front post treble crochet (FPtr): Yarn over, insert the hook from front to back then to the front around the post of the next stitch, yarn over and draw up a loop, (yarn over and draw through two loops) twice.

Back post treble crochet (BPtr): Yarn over, insert the hook from back to front then to the back around the post of the next stitch, yarn over and draw up a loop, (yarn over and draw through two loops) twice.

Designed by
**Donna Jones**

Donna designs, edits and teaches yarn crafts. She believes creative expression is essential for our well-being and aims to instil this in others. Follow her on Instagram @djonesdesigns www.donnajonesdesigns.co.uk

## Pattern

Cut 64 lengths of yarn each measuring 60cm long and set aside for the fringe/tassels.

### Scarf

Using 12mm hook, and your chosen col, ch 19.

Foundation Row: 1 tr into 4th ch from hook (counts as 2 tr), 1 tr into every ch to end, turn. (17 sts)

Row 1 (RS): ch 2 (counts as 1 st), miss st at base of ch, (1 FPtr into next tr, 1 BPtr into next tr) 7 times, 1 FPtr into next tr, 1 tr into 3rd of ch 3, turn.

Row 2: ch 2 (counts as 1 st), miss st at base of ch, (1 BPtr into next tr, 1 FPtr into next tr) 7 times, 1 BPtr into next tr, 1 tr into 3rd of ch 3, turn.

These 2 rows form rib pattern. Repeat these 2 rows until work measures 210cm (82¾in), or your desired length.
Fasten off.

### Fringe

Holding 2 of your pre-cut tassel lengths together, fold in half. With RS facing, and spacing tassels evenly as you work, insert your crochet hook from back to front through the short edge of scarf. Hook the midpoint of the folded fringe strands and draw the loop through the edge. Pull the ends through the loop and tighten. Continue adding tassels in this way until all 16 have been made. Repeat for the other end of the scarf. Trim with scissors to straighten the edge of the fringe.

### Finishing

Spray block and leave to dry completely before unpinning.

Note: Don't be tempted to skip this stage, it makes a considerable difference to how the scarf sits when worn and is well worth the effort!

# Granny square flower scarf

Greet spring's arrival with this pretty scarf of granny square flowers

## Difficulty

★★★☆☆

## What you need

- 4mm hook (US G/6)
- Yarn needle
- Sharp scissors
- You will need to use DK weight yarn, in your chosen colours. We have used Paintbox Yarns in:
  Colour 1: Daffodil Yellow (50g)
  Colour 2: Red Wine (50g)
  Colour 3: Grass Green (50g)
  Colour 4: Banana Cream (150g)

## Measurements

12cm x 173 cm (without fringe), 198 cm (with fringe).

## Special stitches

Popcorn stitch: Work 3 tr into 1 st, work 3 tr into next st, remove hook from working loop, insert hook through both loops of first tr and pull working loop through.

Standing dc: With slipknot already on hook, insert hook into stitch, yo & draw up a loop, then yo and pull through both loops on hook.

Designed by
**Shelley Husband**

Shelley is a long time crafter whose passion is designing crochet patterns. She lives with her husband and teenage daughters in a tiny town on the coast of Victoria, Australia. www.spincushions.com

## Pattern

The Granny Square Flower Scarf is made by joining 12 Granny Square Flowers into a strip then adding a cute fringed edge. There are 2 patterns you can use. The first is easiest, made using only the most basic stitches and the second uses Popcorn stitches for a different look.

### Flower 1

Using 4mm hook with col 1, make a magic ring (alternatively ch 4, and join with ss to form a ring).

Rnd 1: ch 3 (counts as 1 tr), ch 2, *1 tr into ring, ch 2; rep from * 7 times, join with ss to 3rd ch of 3 ch. (8 sts and 8 ch-2 spaces)
Fasten off and weave in ends.

Rnd 2: Using col 2, join with standing dc to any st, *(ss, 3 ch, 3 tr, 3 ch, ss) in next ch-2 space**, dc in next st; rep from * 6 times and from * to ** once, join with ss to standing dc. (8 petals and 8 sts between petals)
Fasten off yarn and weave in ends.

Rnd 3: Using col 3, join with standing dc to any st between petals, *ch 3, skip next petal**, dc in next st; rep from * 6 times and from * to ** once, join with ss to standing dc. (8 sts and 8 ch-3 sps )

Rnd 4: dc in same sp as ss, *(ss, ch 4, 3 dtr, ch 4, ss) in next ch-3 sp**, dc in next st; rep from * 6 times and from * to ** once, join with ss to first dc. (8 leaves and 8 sts between leaves)
Fasten off yarn and weave in ends.

Rnd 5: Using col 4, join with a standing dc to any st between leaves, *ch 3, skip next leaf**, dc in next st; rep from * 6 times and from * to ** once, join with ss to standing dc. (8 sts and 8 ch-3 sps)

Rnd 6: ch 3 (counts as 1 tr), 2 tr in same sp as ss, * ch 1, skip next ch-3 sp, 3 tr in next st, ch 1, skip next 3 ch sp**, (3 tr, ch 2, 3 tr) in next st; rep from * twice and from * to ** once, 3 tr in same sp as first sts, ch 1, join with dc to 3rd ch of 3 ch. (9 sts and 2 ch-1 sps along each side, and 4 corner ch-2 sps)

Rnd 7: ch 3 (counts as 1 tr), 2 tr over joining dc, *[ch 1, skip next 3 sts, 3 tr in next ch-1 sp] twice, ch 1, skip next 3 sts**, (3 tr, ch 2, 3 tr) in next ch-2 sp; rep from * twice and from * to ** once, 3 tr in same sp as first sts, ch 1, join with dc into 3rd ch of 3 ch. (12 sts and 3 ch-1 sps along each side, and 4 corner ch-2 sps)

Rnd 8: ch 3 (counts as 1 tr), 2 tr over joining dc, *(ch 1, skip next 3 sts, 3 tr in ch-1 sp) 3 times, ch 1, skip next 3 sts**, (3 tr, ch 2, 3 tr) in next ch-2 sp; rep from * twice and from * to ** once, 3 tr in same sp as first sts, ch 1, join with dc into 3rd ch of 3 ch. (15 sts and 4 ch-1 sps along each side, and 4 corner ch-2 sps)

Rnd 9: dc over joining dc, *(dc in next 3 sts, dc in next 1-ch sp) 4 times, dc in next 3 sts**, (dc, ch 2, dc) in next ch-2 sp; rep from * twice and from * to ** once, dc in same sp as first dc, ch 2, join with ss to first dc. (21 sts along each side and 4 corner ch-2 sps)
Fasten off and weave in ends.

### Flower 2

Using col 1, make a magic ring (alternatively ch 4, and join with ss to form a ring).

Rnd 1: ch 3 (counts as 1 tr), 15 tr into ring,

join with ss to 3rd ch of 3 ch. (16 sts)
Fasten off and weave in ends.

**Rnd 2:** Using col 2, join with a standing tr to any st, *pc in next st**, tr in next st; rep from * 6 times and from * to ** once, join with ss to standing tr. (16 sts)
Fasten off yarn and weave in ends.

**Rnd 3:** Using col 3, join with a standing dc to any tr of Rnd 2, *ch 3, skip next pc**, dc in next st; rep from * 6 times and from * to ** once, join with ss to standing dc. (8 sts and 8 ch-3 sps)

**Rnd 4:** ch 3 (counts as 1 tr), (2 tr, ch 2, 3 tr) in same sp as ss, *dc in next ch-3 sp**, (3 tr, ch 2, 3 tr) in next st; rep from * 6 times and from * to ** once, join with ss to 3rd ch of 3 ch. (8 leaves and 8 sts between leaves)
Fasten off and weave in ends.

**Rnd 5:** Using col 4, join with standing dc to any st between leaves, *ch 4, skip next leaf**, dc in next st; rep from * 6 times and from * to ** once, join with ss to standing dc.
(8 sts and 8 ch-4 sps)

**Rnd 6:** ch 3 (counts as 1 tr), 2 tr in same sp as ss, * ch 1, skip next ch-4 sp, 3 tr in next st, ch 1, skip next ch-4 sp**, (3 tr, ch 2, 3 tr) in next st; rep from * twice and from * to ** once, 3 tr in same sp as first sts, ch 1, join with dc to 3rd ch of 3 ch. (9 sts and 2 ch-1 sps along each side, and 4 corner ch-2 sps)

**Rnd 7:** ch 3 (counts as 1 tr), 2 tr over joining dc, *(ch 1, skip next 3 sts, 3 tr in next ch-1 sp) twice, ch 1, skip next 3 sts**, (3 tr, ch 2, 3 tr) in next corner ch-2 sp; rep from * twice and from * to ** once, 3 tr in same sp as first sts, ch 1, join with dc into 3rd ch of 3 ch. (12 sts and 3 ch-1 sps along each side, and 4 corner ch-2 sps)

**Rnd 8:** ch 3 (counts as 1 tr), 2 tr over joining dc, *(ch 1, skip next 3 sts, 3 tr in next ch-1 sp) 3 times, ch 1, skip next 3 sts**, (3 tr, ch 2, 3 tr) in next corner ch-2 sp; rep from * twice and from * to ** once, 3 tr in same sp as first sts, ch 1, join with dc into 3rd ch of 3 ch. (15 sts and 4 ch-1 sps along each side, and 4 corner ch-2 sps)

**Rnd 9:** dc over joining dc, *(dc in next 3 sts, dc in next ch-1 sp) 4 times, dc in next 3 sts**, (dc, ch 2, dc) in next corner ch-2 sp; rep from * twice and from * to ** once, dc in same sp as first dc, ch 2, join with ss to first dc. (21 sts along each side and 4 corner ch-2 sps)
Fasten off and weave in ends.

## Finishing

Join all 12 squares in a strip by holding 2 squares right sides together. Join col 4 with a standing dc to the corner ch-2 sps of both squares, dc in 21 sts of both squares at the same time, dc in corner ch-2 sps of both squares.

Fasten off yarn and weave in ends.

Cut 46 30cm lengths of col 4 and attach one to each st and corner ch-2 sp along the bottom edges.

# Long wave neckwarmer

There's nothing like a good, blustery walk by the sea on a cold winter's day. Keep warm with this wave-inspired neck warmer

## Difficulty

★★★☆☆

## What you need

- 5mm hook (US H/8)
- Yarn needle
- You will need to use an Aran weight yarn in your chosen colours. We have used Debbie Bliss Cashmerino in:
  Colour 1: Jade, 061; 50g
  Colour 2: Ecru, 101; 50g

## Tension

14 stitches and 12 rows = 10 x 10cm (4 x 4in) over wave pattern using 5mm (US H/8) hook.

## Measurements

The neckwarmer's circumference measures 60cm (23½in) and is 25cm (10in) deep.

## Pattern

### Neckwarmer

Using 5mm hook and col 1 make 84 ch and join in round using sl st, making sure not to twist the chain.

Rnd 1 (Colour 1): ch 2 (counts as 1 dc), *1 dc in next chain, 2 htr in next ch 2, 2 tr in next ch 2, 3 dtr in next ch 3, 2 tr in next ch 2, 2 htr in next ch 2, 2 dc in next ch 2* five times, 1 dc in next chain, 2 htr in next ch 2, 2 tr in next ch 2, 3 dtr in next ch 3, 2 tr in next ch 2, 2 htr in next ch 2, 1 dc in next ch 1, join to 2nd starting ch with sl st.

Rnd 2: ch 2 (counts as 1 dc), dc in every st to end, join to 2nd starting ch with sl st.

Rnd 3 (Colour 2): ch 4 (counts as 1 dtr), *1 dtr, 2 tr,
2 htr, 3 dc, 2 htr, 2 tr, 2 dtr* five times, 1 dtr,
2 tr, 2 htr, 3 dc, 2 htr, 2tr, 1 dtr, join to starting ch with sl st.

Rnd 4: Rep round 2.

Rnd 5 (Colour 1): ch 2 (counts as 1 dc), *1 dc, 2 htr,
2 tr, 3 dtr, 2 tr, 2 htr, 2 dc*
five times, 1 dc, 2 htr, 2 tr, 3 dtr,
2 tr, 2 htr, 1 dc, join to starting ch with sl st.

Rnd 6: Rep round 2.

Rounds 3-6 form the striped wave pattern. Repeat these 4 rounds until neckwarmer measures approx 25cm (10in), ending by repeating rnd 2 (in colour 1).

Fasten off.

### Finishing

Weave in ends and press or block lightly using preferred method and/or following recommendations shown on the ball band of your yarn.

Designed by **Sian Brown**

After doing a Fashion/Textiles BA, Sian worked supplying machine knits to high street retailers. She became interested in handknits and has been designing them ever since, working for magazines, publishers and yarn companies. Her book Knitted Home is available now. www.sianbrown.co.uk

# Honeycomb belle hat

This cute hat uses a bobble stitch to create a thicker fabric that will keep your head nice and warm. Top it off with a big pompom for an on-trend look

## Difficulty

★★★☆☆

## What you need

- 12mm hook (US O/17)
- 1 stitch marker
- Large-eyed tapestry needle/bodkin
- 65mm pompom maker (optional)
- Sharp scissors
- You will need Super Chunky yarn in your chosen colours. We have used Debbie Bliss Roma yarn in:
  Colour 1: Coral, 017; 100g
  Colour 2: Citrus, 08; 100g

## Tension

7.5 stitches and 6 rows = 10 x 10cm (4 x 4in) over honeycomb puff pattern using 12mm (US O/17) hook.

## Measurements

The hat stretches to fit average female head measuring 51cm (20in)
Finished measurements: 44cm (17¼in) around brim, 25.5cm (10in) from crown to edge of brim.

## Special stitches

Honeycomb puff pattern: Consists of dc and bobbles made by working 5 treble sts together.
Half treble rib: A variation of half treble stitch, where the stitches are worked by inserting your hook into the loop directly below the top loop that you would normally work into.

## Pattern

### Rib brim

Using 12 mm hook and col 1 make 6 ch.
Row 1: Skip ch 2 (does not count as st), 1 htr into every ch, to end, turn. (4 sts)
Row 2: ch 2, 1 htr into loop directly below top loops of each htr to end, turn.
Rep row 2 until rib measures approx 44cm (17¼in).

### Main body and crown

Turn work clockwise so that long edge is facing upwards, work 33 dc sts evenly across top of rib, and join to work in the round with a sl st into top of first dc made. Place stitch marker to indicate beg/end of each rnd.
Honeycomb Puff Stitch
Rnd 1: ch 1, 1 dc into base of ch, 1 dc in next dc, *tr5tog, 1 dc in next 2 dc; rep from * to last dc, t5tog, sl st into first dc made.
Rnd 2: ch 1, 1 dc into base of ch, 1 dc in next dc, * 1 dc in top of tr5tog, 1 dc in next 2 dc; rep from * to last st, 1 dc in top of tr5tog, sl st into first dc made.
Rnd 3: ch 1, *tr5tog in next dc, 1 dc in next 2 dc; rep from * to end, sl st in top of first tr5tog made.
Rnd 4: ch 1, *1 dc in top of tr5tog, 1 dc in next 2 dc; rep from * to end, sl st into first dc made.
Rnds 5-7: Rep Rnds 1-3.
Change to col 2.
Rnd 8: Rep Rnd 4.
Rnd 9: Rep Rnd 1.
Rnd 10 (dec): ch 1, 1 dc in base of ch, *skip 1 dc, 1 dc in next 2 dc; rep from * to last 2 sts, skip 1 dc, 1 dc, sl st into first dc made. (22 sts)
Rnd 11: ch 1, *tr5tog in next dc, 1 dc in next dc; rep from * to end, sl st into first tr5tog made.
Rnd 12: ch 1, *1 dc in top of tr5tog, 1dc in next dc; rep from * to end sl st into first dc made.
Rnd 13 (dec): ch 1, 1 dc in base ch, *skip 1 dc, 1 dc in next dc; rep from * to last dc, skip 1 dc, sl st into first dc made. (11 sts)
Rnd 14 (dec): ch 1, 1 dc in base, *skip 1, 1 dc in next dc; rep from * to last 2 dc, skip 2 dc, sl st into first dc made.
5 sts. Fasten off.
Use a running stitch around the top of the crown, pull gently to drawn in and close.

## Finishing

Join rib seam neatly and fasten off any loose ends. Using col 2 make a 65mm pompom and join to centre of crown.

## Designed by Emma Wright

Emma is a designer with a passion for British fashion, flowers and her home county of Yorkshire. See more from her at: www.emmaknitted.co.uk Ravelry username: emmaknitsjumpers Twitter: @Emmaknitted Instagram: @Emmaknitted

## Top Tip

The ribbed hem is stretchy so the hat will fit snugly to your head while out on blustery winter walks.

# Scallop-edged hat and cowl

This simple hat and cowl pattern uses basic crochet stitches, works up quickly, and the scallop edge adds a fun touch!

## Difficulty

## What you need

- 9mm hook (US M/13)
- 6.5mm hook (US K/10.5)
- Cardboard (or pom pom maker)
- Fabric glue (optional)
- You will need chunky weight yarn in your chosen colours. We have used Bernat Softee Chunky in:
  Colour 1: Clay (300g per item)
  Colour 2: White (100g per item)

## Tension

Using Chunky Yarn and 9mm Hook:
Row 1: ch 11, 1 tr in 3rd ch from hook and in each across, turn. (9sts).
Row 2: ch 2 (does not count as st), 1 tr in each st. Piece should measure approximately 10cm x 5cm.

## Measurements

Hat: 27cm x 23cm Scarf: 69cm x 20cm

Designed by
**Jenni Catavu**

Jenni Catavu is a self-taught crocheter and designer residing in Wisconsin, USA where she enjoys hiking and spending time exploring the outdoors with her family. www.byjennidesigns.com

## Pattern

### Hat

Using a 9mm hook in col 1, make a magic ring.
Rnd 1: ch 2, 10 tr into ring, join with ss. (10 sts)
Rnd 2: ch 2, 1 tr in first st, 2 tr in each st to end, join with ss. (19 sts)
Rnd 3: ch 2, 1 tr in first st, *2 tr in next st, 1 tr in next st; rep from * to end, join with ss. (28 sts)
Rnd 4: ch 2, 1 tr in first st, *2 tr in next st, 1 tr in next 2 sts; rep from * to end, join with ss. (37 sts)
Rnd 5: ch 2, 1 tr in first st, *2 tr in next st, 1 tr in next 8 sts; rep from * to end, join with ss. (41 sts)
Rnds 6-10: ch 2, 1 tr in each st, join with ss. (41 sts)
Rnd 11: ch 1, 1 htr in each st, join with ss. (41 sts)
Rnd 12: ch 1, 1 dc in each st, join with ss. (ss counts as a st in this rnd only). (42 sts)
Fasten off.

### Hat edging

Using a 6.5mm hook in col 2 join with ss in any st from rnd 12.
Next Rnd: *ch 3, skip 1, ss in next st; rep from * to end, join with ss.
Fasten off.
Note: Remember that the ss from Rnd 12 counts as a stitch here.

### Pompom

Using col 2 cut a 61cm length of yarn and lay it on a flat surface and set aside.
1. Using a 10cm x 10cm piece of cardboard wrap yarn around cardboard about 60 times.
2. Carefully slip the yarn off the cardboard and lay on top of the 61cm length of yarn. Tie a double knot around the middle to secure. Using the long ends of the length of yarn and a tapestry needle sew in and out of the center of the pompom to hold it together firmly (note: for an extra secure pompom run a line of fabric glue across the center, let dry). Alternatively use a commercial pompom maker for ease if you have one.
3. Cut through all the loops and trim the pompom up until it's even and looks neat.

### Finishing

Sew your pompom to the top of the hat and weave in all the ends.

## Pattern

### Cowl

Using a 9mm hook in col 1, ch 124 and join in round with ss to the first ch taking care not to twist the chain.
Rnd 1: ch 2, 1 tr in same ch as ss and 1 tr in each ch to end, join with ss. (124 sts)
Rnds 2-8: ch 2, 1 tr in each st, join with ss. (124 sts)
Fasten off.

### Cowl edging

Using a 6.5mm hook in col 2 join with ss in first tr of Rnd 8.
Edging Rnd: *Ch 4, skip 1, ss in next st; rep from * to end, join with ss.
Fasten off.

Join with ss in any tr on the opposite edge of the scarf and work edging rnd as above.
Fasten off.

### Finishing

Weave in all the ends.

Designed by
**Joleen Kraft**

Joleen is an herbalist in Victoria, BC, Canada. An enthusiastic knitter and crocheter, she began designing patterns in 2012. She is kept company by her partner, Chris, and her cat, Ivan.
www.kraftling.ca

# Boho poncho

An easy-to-crochet poncho featuring a lacy stitch, it hangs beautifully, making it a staple item in any closet

## Difficulty

★★★☆☆

## What you need

- 6.5 mm hook (US K/10.5)
- You will need to use a chunky weight yarn in your chosen colour. Here we have used Berroco Vintage Chunky yarn. For sizes S [M : L] you will need: 300g [400g : 500g]

## Tension

11 stitches and 12 rows = 10cm x 10cm over dc using 6.5mm hook tension.

## Measurements

Child: 33 x 51cm
Medium: 43 x 71cm
Large: 53.5 x 81.5cm

## Special stitches

Puff stitch: Yarn over and insert hook into next st. Draw up a loop but don't pull through the working loops, instead pull the loop up to the desired height. *Yarn over and insert hook into the same stitch and draw up another loop, pulling it up to match the height.* 2 times. You should have 7 loops on your hook. Yarn over and pull through all 7 loops. Ch 1 to close the puff stitch.

# Pattern

## Rectangle (make 2)

Using 6.5mm hook, ch 40 [52 : 64].

Row 1: (1 tr, ch 2, 1 tr) in 4th ch from hook, *skip 2 ch, 1 puff st in next ch, skip 2 ch, (1 tr, ch 2, 1 tr) in next ch; rep from * to end, turn. (7 [9 : 11] ch-2 sps and 6 [8 : 10] puff sts.)

Row 2: ch 3, *1 puff st in ch-2 sp between 2 tr of previous row, (1 tr, ch 2, 1 tr) in top of next puff st; rep from * to last ch-2 sp, make 1 puff st in ch-2 sp, 1 tr in 3rd ch of 3 ch, turn. (7 [9 : 11] puff sts and 6 [8 : 10] ch-2 sps.)

Row 3: ch 3, (1 tr, ch 2, 1 tr) in top of next puff st, *1 puff in ch-2 sp, (1 tr, ch 2, 1 tr) in top of next puff st; rep from * to last puff st, (1 tr, ch 2, 1 tr) in top of puff st and 1 tr in 3rd ch of 3 ch, turn. (7 [9 : 11] ch-2 sps and 6 [8 : 10] puff sts.)

Rep rows 2 and 3 until a total of 25 [35 : 40] rows have been completed.

## Assembly

Lay the two completed rectangles side by side as shown in illustration.

With wrong sides facing pin short edge along bottom of rectangle A to dotted line indicated on rectangle B (which is approximately 10 [21 : 26] rows). Join with double crochet into each st along short edge of A, working approximately 5 sts to 2 row edges along B.

## Finishing

Weave in all ends and block.



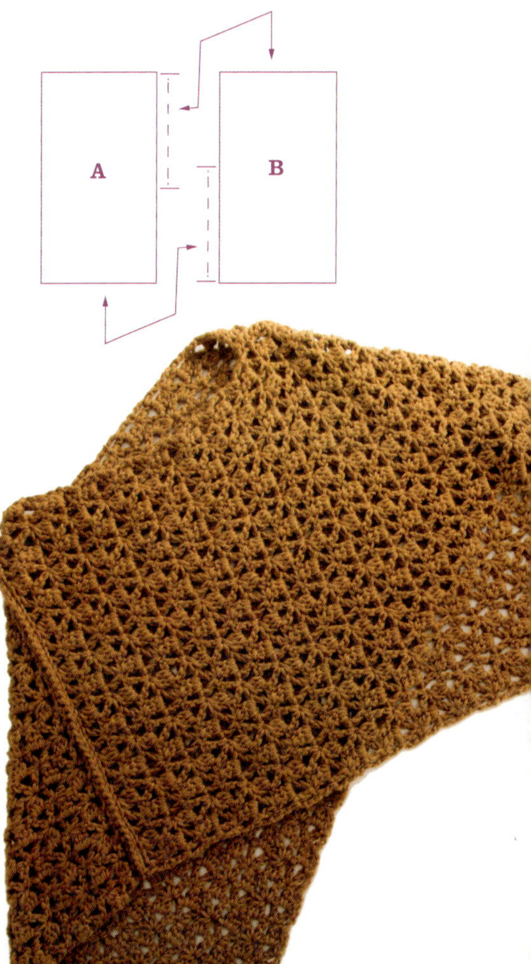

# A cute sweater

The clever use of triangles creates flattering lines in the body of this sweater and makes for a quick and easy project

## Difficulty

★★★★☆

## What you need

- 5.5mm hook (US H/8)
- 6mm hook (US J/10)
- 2 buttons (optional)
- Yarn needle (optional)
- You will need to use a DK yarn in your chosen colour. You will need approximately 3 [4 : 4 : 5] skeins

## Measurements

Sizes S/M/L/XL Choose the size that best matches you or the recipient's actual bust measurement plus a couple of inches to spare for ease

Bust: 79.5 [90 : 100 : 113.5]cm

Length (excluding collar): 48.5[52 : 56 : 61]cm

Length sleeve seam: 51.5[56.5 : 61.5 : 64]cm

## Special stitches

Bobble cluster: (yo, insert hook, draw up a loop) 3 times in same st, yo and draw through 7 loops on hook.

# Pattern

## Bobble triangle (make 2)

Using 5.5mm hook, ch 4.

Row 1: 1 dc in 2nd ch from hook, make bobble cluster in next ch, 1 dc in last ch, turn. (3 sts)

Row 2: ch 1, 2 dc in first st, 1 dc in each st to last st, 2 dc in last st, turn. (5 sts)

Row 3: ch 1, 1 dc in next st, *make bobble cluster in next st, 1 dc in next st; rep from * to end, turn. (5 sts)

Rep rows 2 and 3 inc 1 st at each end on alternate rows as set until 47 [53 : 59 : 67] sts rem, ending with a row 3 (and a total of 45 [51 : 57 : 65] rows have been worked).

Dec row: ch 1, dc2tog, 1 dc in each st to last 2 sts, dc2tog, turn. (45 [51 : 57 : 65] sts)

Next row: ch 1, 1 dc in next st, *make bobble cluster in next st, 1 dc in next st; rep from * to end, turn. (45 [51 : 57 : 65] sts)

Rep last two rows decreasing by 2 sts on alternate rows as set until 27 [33 : 39 : 47] sts rem, ending with a bobble cluster row (and 20 rows have been worked).

Fasten off.

## Side triangle (make 2)

Using 5.5mm hook, ch 4.

Row 1: 1 dc in 2nd ch from hook, 1 dc in each ch to end, turn. (3 sts)

Row 2: ch 1, 2 dc in first st, 1 dc in each st to last st, 2 dc in last st, turn. (5 sts)

Row 3: ch 1, 1 dc in each st to end, turn. (5 sts)

Rep rows 2 and 3 inc 1 st at each end on alternate rows as set until 47 [57 : 65 : 73] sts rem ending with a row 3 (and total of 45 [55 : 63 : 71] rows have been worked).

Fasten off.

## Joining body

Take a side triangle and one of the bobble triangles and place side by side. Place the side triangle so its longest row is next to the diagonal edge of the bobble triangle, and then dc or sew seam on WS of fabric, gently easing the edges to fit together evenly across the seam (seams are worked on the inside of the sweater). Repeat so that the row ends edge of the same triangle is attached to the second bobble triangle as shown in diagram.

Repeat with second side triangle by seaming in place in the same way, making sure to mirror the direction of the rows of the other side triangle.

## Sleeves (make 2)

Sleeves are worked from the top down towards the wrist.

Using 5.5mm hook, ch 21 [25 : 29 : 33].

Row 1: 1 dc in 2nd ch from hook, 1 dc in each ch to end, turn. (20 [24 : 28 : 32] sts)

Row 2: ch 1, 2 dc in first st, 1 dc in each st to last st, 2 dc in last st, turn. (22 [26 : 30 : 34] sts)

Row 3: ch 1, 1 dc in each st to end, turn. (22 [26 : 30 : 34] sts)

Rep rows 2 and 3 inc 1 st at each end on alternate rows as set until 40 [44 : 48 : 52] sts rem ending with a row 2 (and 20 rows have been worked).

Place a marker at each end of last row.

Next 4 rows: ch 1, 1 dc in each st to end, turn. (40 [44 : 48 : 52] sts)

Dec row: ch 1, dc2tog, 1 dc in each st to last 2 sts, dc2tog, turn. (38 [42 : 46 : 50] sts)

Next 5 rows: ch 1, 1 dc in each st to end, turn. (38 [42 : 46 : 50] sts)

Rep last 6 rows until 20 [22 : 24 : 28] sts rem, ending with a dec row.

Work a further 2 rows straight in dc.

Fasten off.

## Joining sleeves

Beginning 12 rows up from wrist end of sleeve, seam sleeves from this point to the markers. Pin sleeve in place in armhole of sweater body and then dc or sew in place (diagonal edges of upper sleeves to fit with upper diagonal edges of bobble triangles). The top row of the sleeve (first row worked) creates the shoulder width between front and back and is not seamed when stitching sleeve in place.

## Collar

Choose the front and back of the sweater. You're now going to be working in the round to add the collar, working into the back loops only of the stitches in row below. With RS facing and using 5.5mm hook, attach yarn to left back shoulder seam.

Rnds 1-2 (blo): ch 1, 1 dc in each st around neck to end, join with ss to first dc, turn. (2 rnds worked)

Rnd 3 (blo): ch 1, dec 4 [4 : 5 : 5] sts evenly across left sleeve top by working (dc2tog, 1 dc in each of next 3 sts) 4 [4 : 5 : 5] times, dc in each st across front neck, dec 4 [4 : 5 : 5] sts evenly across right sleeve top as before, dc in each st across back neck to end, join with ss to first dc, turn.

Note: These decreases are for shaping over

the shoulder and their placement does not need to be precise.

Rnd 4: ch 1, 1 dc in each st to end, join with ss to first dc, turn.
Rnd 5: ch 1, dec 4 [4 : 5 : 5] sts evenly across left sleeve top by working (dc2tog, 1 dc in each of next 2 sts) 4 [4 : 5 : 5] times, dc in each st across front neck, dec 4 [4 : 5 : 5] sts evenly across right sleeve top as before, dc in each st to to end, join with ss to first dc, turn.
Rnds 6-14: ch 1, 1 dc in each st around neck to end, join with ss to first dc, turn. (9 nds worked)
Fasten off.

## Bottom hem

You're now going to be working in the round to add the hem, working into the back loops only of the stitches below.
With RS facing and using a 6mm hook attach yarn to bottom point of bobble triangle at back of sweater.
Rnd 1: (blo): ch 1, 1 dc in each st or dc row edge to end, join with ss to first dc, turn.
Rnds 2-10 (blo): ch 1, 1 dc in each st to end, join with ss to first dc, turn. (9 rnds worked)
Fasten off.

## Finishing

Weave in all loose ends and block sweater if desired. If using buttons, attach one at end of each sleeve. With 5.5mm hook ch 10 (or length required to slip around button) and attach the chained length to the opposite edge of sleeve to form a button loop. Fold up sleeve end or leave down

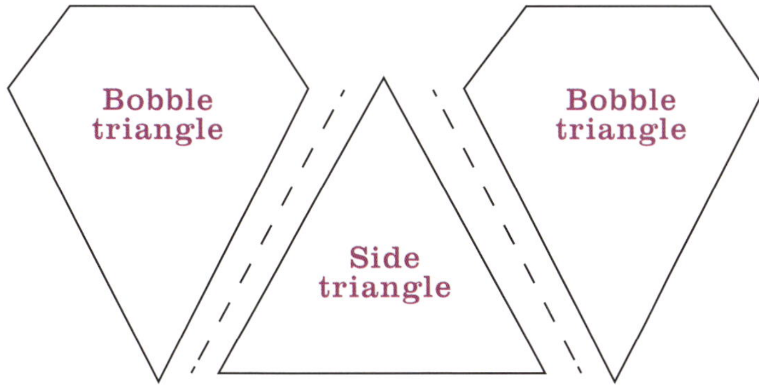


**Designed by**

## Joleen Kraft

Joleen is an herbalist in Victoria, BC, Canada. An enthusiastic knitter and crocheter, she began designing patterns in 2012. She is kept company by her partner, Chris, and her cat, Ivan.
www.kraftling.ca

# Squares baby blanket

A comfy creation to keep your little one warm and cozy

## Difficulty

★★★☆☆

## What you need

- 4mm hook (US G/6)
- Yarn needle
- You will need to use DK weight yarn, in your chosen colours. Here we have used Sublime Baby Cashmere Merino Silk DK in:

MC (main colour): Pebble, 006 (400g)
CC (contrast colours):
Colour 1: Vanilla, 003 (100g)
Colour 2: Bounty blue, 493 (100g)
Colour 3: Little Lobby, 94 (100g)
Colour 4: Pip, 381 (100g

## Tension

One square to measure 12 x 12cm (4¾ x 4¾in) using 4mm (US G/6) crochet hook, or size required to obtain correct tension.

## Measurements

80cm x 80cm (31½in x 31½in).

## Special stitches

Crab stitch/reverse dc: Yo and draw up a loop, making sure your hook faces left as it would usually. Complete the stitch as normal and then continue to work backwards along your edge. Make sure not to twist your hook!

Designed by
**Donna Jones**

Donna designs, edits and teaches yarn crafts. She believes creative expression is essential for our well-being and aims to instil this in others. Follow her on Instagram @djonesdesigns www.donnajonesdesigns.co.uk

## Pattern

### Square 1 - Granny in the middle

(Make 12 squares – 1 in each of the 12 colour combinations, see pattern notes)
Using MC, make 4 ch and join with sl st to form a ring.

Rnd 1 (MC): ch 3 (counts as 1 tr), 2 tr into ring, ch 2, (3 tr into ring, ch 2) 3 times, join with sl st in third ch of ch 3. Fasten off.

Rnd 2 (CC1): Join CC1 in any corner ch 2 sp. ch 3 (counts as 1 tr), (2 tr, ch 2, 3 tr) into same ch 2 sp, *ch 1, (3 tr, ch 2, 3 tr) into next ch 2 sp; rep from * twice more, ch 1, join with sl st in third ch of ch 3. Fasten off.

Rnd 3 (CC2): Join CC2 in any corner ch 2 sp. ch 3 (counts as 1 tr), (2 tr, ch 2, 3 tr) into same ch 2 sp, *ch 1, 3 tr into next ch 1 sp, ch 1, (3 tr, ch 2, 3 tr) into next corner ch 2 sp; rep from * twice more, 3 tr into next edge ch sp, ch 1, join with sl st in third ch of ch 3. Do not fasten off.

Rnd 4 (CC2): sl st into each of next 2 tr and into next corner ch 2 sp. ch 3 (counts as 1 tr), (2 tr, ch 2, 3 tr) into same ch 2 sp, *(ch 1, 3 tr into next ch 1 sp) twice, ch 1, (3 tr, ch 2, 3 tr) into next corner ch 2 sp; rep from * twice more, (ch 1, 3 tr into next ch 1 sp) twice, ch 1, join with sl st in third ch of ch 3. Fasten off.

Rnd 5 (MC): Join MC in any corner ch 2 sp. ch 3 (counts as 1 tr), (1 tr, ch 2, 2 tr) into same ch 2 sp, *(1 tr into each of next 3 tr, 1 tr into next ch 1 sp) 3 times, 1 tr into each of next 3 tr, (2 tr, ch 2, 2 tr) into corner ch 2 sp; rep from * twice more, (1 tr into each of next 3 tr, 1 tr into next ch 1 sp) 3 times, 1 tr into each of next 3 tr, join with sl st into third ch of ch 3. Do not fasten off.

Rnd 6 (MC): ch 1 (does not count as st), 1 dc into each tr of prev round, working 5 dc into each corner ch 2 sp, join with sl st into first dc. Do not fasten off.

Rnd 7 (MC): ch 1 (does not count as st), 1 dc into each dc of prev round, working 3 dc into centre of 5 dc corner group, join with sl st into first dc. Fasten off.

### Square 2 - Circle in a square

(Make 12 squares – 1 in each of the 12 colour combinations)
Using MC, work 4 ch and join with sl st to form a ring.

Rnd 1 (MC): ch 3 (counts as 1 tr), 15 tr into ring, join with sl st into third ch of ch 3. Fasten off.

Rnd 2 (CC1): Join CC1 in sp between any 2 tr. ch 3 (counts as 1 tr), 1 tr into same sp, 2 tr into sp between each rem tr of prev round, join with sl st into third ch of ch 3. Fasten off.

Rnd 3 (CC2): Change to CC2. ch 3 (counts as 1 tr), 1 tr into same place, 1 tr into next tr, (2 tr into next tr, 1 tr into next tr) 15 times, join with sl st into third ch of ch 3. Do not fasten off.

Rnd 4 (CC2): ch 4 (counts as 1 dtr), (2 tr, ch 2, 2 tr, 1 dtr) into same tr, *miss 1 tr, 1 htr into each of next 3 tr, 1 dc into each of next 3 tr, 1 htr into each of next 3 tr, miss next tr, (1 dtr, 2 tr, ch 2, 2 tr, 1 dtr) into next tr; rep from * twice more, miss 1 tr, 1 htr into each of next 3 tr, 1 dc into each of next 3 tr, 1 htr into each of next 3 tr, miss next tr, join with sl st into fourth ch of ch 4. Fasten off.

Rnd 5 (MC): Join MC into any corner ch 2 sp. ch 3 (counts as 1 tr), (1 tr, ch 2, 2 tr) into same sp, *1 tr into each of next 15 sts, (2 tr, ch 2, 2 tr) into corner ch 2 sp; rep from * twice more, 1 tr into each of next 15 sts, join with sl st into third ch of ch 3. Do not fasten off.

Rnd 6 (MC): ch 1 (does not count as st), 1 dc into each tr of prev round, working 5 dc into each corner ch 2 sp, join with sl st into first dc.

Rnd 7 (MC): ch 1 (does not count as st), 1 dc into each dc of prev round, working 3 dc into centre of 5 dc corner group, join with sl st into first dc. Fasten off.

## Square 3 - Solid squares

(Make 12 squares – 1 in each of the 12 colour combinations)

Using MC, work 4 ch and join with sl st to form a ring.

Rnd 1 (MC): ch 3 (counts as 1 tr), 2 tr into ring, ch 2, (3 tr into ring, ch 2) 3 times, join with sl st into third ch of ch 3. Fasten off.

Rnd 2 (CC1): Join CC1 in any corner ch 2 sp. ch 3 (counts as 1 tr), (1 tr, ch 2, 2 tr) into same ch 2 sp, *1 tr into each of next 3 tr, (2 tr, ch 2, 2 tr) into next ch 2 sp; rep from * twice more, 1 tr into each of next 3 tr, join with sl st into third ch of ch 3, do not fasten off.

Rnd 3 (CC1): Sl st into next tr and into next corner ch 2 sp, ch 3 (counts as 1 tr), (1 tr, ch 2, 2 tr) into same ch 2 sp, *1 tr into each of next 7 tr, (2 tr, ch 2, 2 tr) into next ch 2 sp; rep from * twice more, 1 tr into each of next 7 tr, join with sl st into third ch of ch 3. Fasten off.

Rnd 4 (CC2): Join CC2 in any corner ch 2 sp, ch 3 (counts as 1 tr), (1 tr, ch 2, 2 tr) into same ch 2 sp, *1 tr into each of next 11 tr, (2 tr, ch 2, 2 tr) into next ch 2 sp; rep from * twice more, 1 tr into each of next 11 tr, join with sl st into third ch of ch 3, fasten off.

Rnd 5 (MC): Join MC in any corner ch 2 sp, ch 3 (counts as 1 tr), (1 tr, ch 2, 2 tr) into same ch 2 sp, *1 tr into each of next 15 tr, (2 tr, ch 2, 2 tr) into next ch 2 sp; rep from * twice more, 1 tr into each of next 15 tr, join with sl st into third ch of ch 3. Fasten off.

Rnd 6 (MC): ch 1 (does not count as st), 1 dc into each tr of prev round, working 5 dc into each corner ch 2 sp, join with sl st into first dc.

Rnd 7 (MC): ch 1 (does not count as st), 1 dc into each dc of prev round, working 3 dc into centre of 5 dc corner group, join with sl st into first dc. Fasten off.

## Making up

Weave in all loose ends. Place the squares in 6 rows of 6 squares each, moving the order about until you are pleased with the layout. Make a note of this layout so that you can refer to this as you assemble the blanket. Using MC and the flat slip-stitched seam technique, join the squares into strips of 6, then join these 6 strips together to form the blanket.

## Border

With RS facing, join MC in any edge dc.

Rnd 1: ch 1 (does not count as st), 1 dc into each dc around edge, working 3 dc into centre st of 3 dc at each corner, join with sl st into first dc.

Rnds 2-3: Rep Round 1.

Rnd 4: Crab stitch edging - ch 1 (does not count as st), 1 rev dc into each dc around edge, working 3 rev dc into each corner, join with sl st into first rev dc. Fasten off.

## Finishing

Weave in all ends and block.

### Pattern notes

- Weaving in the ends as you complete each square will make piecing your blanket together much quicker.
- Blocking makes a huge difference to the finish and handle of the blanket, and is well worth the effort.
- There are 12 colour combinations for each square: Rounds 1, 5, 6 and 7 are always worked with MC. For the feature rounds use the following combinations:

| CC1 | CC2 |
|---|---|
| 1: Colour 1 | Colour 2 |
| 2: Colour 1 | Colour 3 |
| 3: Colour 1 | Colour 4 |
| 4: Colour 2 | Colour 1 |
| 5: Colour 2 | Colour 3 |
| 6: Colour 2 | Colour 4 |
| 7: Colour 3 | Colour 1 |
| 8: Colour 3 | Colour 2 |
| 9: Colour 3 | Colour 4 |
| 10: Colour 4 | Colour 1 |
| 11: Colour 4 | Colour 2 |
| 12: Colour 4 | Colour 3 |

# Hushabye sleeping bag

Reminiscent of homely 'granny' squares, this simple sleeping bag is perfect for newborn babies to snuggle up in

## Difficulty

★★★☆☆

## What you need

- 4mm hook (US G/6)
- 10 x 2.5cm (1 in) buttons
- You will need DK weight yarn in your chosen colours. We have used Sublime Baby Cashmere Merino Silk DK in:
  Colour 1: Pebble (250g)
  Colour 2: Vanilla (100g)
  Colour 3: Splash (50g)

## Tension

Tension is not critical for this project, but if you do not match it your sleeping bag will vary in size to that stated and you may need more yarn. 5 pattern repeats and 11 rows measure 10cm square, using 4mm hook.

## Measurements

Sleeping Bag measures 37cm wide and 44cm long excluding hood. Hood measures approx 23cm from top of bag to point.

## Special stitches

Crab stitch/reverse dc: Yo and draw up a loop, making sure your hook faces left as it would usually. Complete the stitch as normal and then continue to work backwards along your edge. Make sure not to twist your hook!

## Pattern

### Front

Using 4mm hook and col 1, ch 55.

Row 1 (RS): 3 tr in 7th ch from hook, *miss 2 ch, 3 tr in next ch; rep from * to last 3 ch, miss 2 ch, tr in last st, turn. Place a marker at the end of this row to mark fold line. (16 treble clusters and 2 edge sts)

Row 2: ch 3 (counts as 1st tr), 1 tr in ch-sp before next treble cluster, *3 tr in each space between treble clusters along the row to last ch-sp, 2 tr in last ch-sp, turn. (15 treble clusters with 2 half clusters)

Row 3: ch 3 (counts as 1st tr), 3 tr in each space between treble clusters along the row to last 2 tr, skip next tr, 1 tr in top of beginning ch 3 of previous row. (16 treble clusters and 2 edge sts)

Rows 2 and 3 form pattern. Cont working in pattern for remainder of piece, working in stripes as follows:

Rows 4-5: 2 rows with col 1.
Row 6: 1 row with col 2.
Rows 7-8: 2 rows with col 1.
Rows 9-11: 3 rows with col 3.
Rows 12-13: 2 rows with col 1.
Row 14: 1 row with col 2.
Rows 15-19: 5 rows with col 1.
Row 20: 1 row with col 3.
Rows 21-22: 2 rows with col 1.
Rows 23-25: 3 rows with col 2.
Rows 26-27: 2 rows with col 1.
Row 28: 1 row with col 3.
Rows 29-33: 5 rows with col 1.
Row 34: 1 row with col 2.
Rows 35-36: 2 rows with col 1.
Rows 37-39: 3 rows with col 3.
Rows 40-41: 2 rows with col 1.
Row 42: 1 row with col 2.
Rows 43-44: 2 rows with col 1.
Fasten off.

### Back and hood

Using col 1 and with RS facing, rotate work and fasten on at the marker to begin working along bottom of piece (this will be the fold line along the bottom of the bag). Continue working in pattern throughout in stripes as follows:

Rows 1-5: 5 rows with col 1.
Row 6: 1 row with col 2.
Rows 7-8: 2 rows with col 1.
Rows 9-11: 3 rows with col 3.
Rows 12-13: 2 rows with col 1.
Row 14: 1 row with col 2.
Rows 15-19: 5 rows with col 1.
Row 20: 1 row with col 3.
Rows 21-22: 2 rows with col 1.
Rows 23-25: 3 rows with col 2.
Rows 26-27: 2 rows with col 1.
Row 28: 1 row with col 3.
Rows 29-33: 5 rows with col 1.
Row 34: 1 row with col 2.
Rows 35-36: 2 rows with col 1.
Rows 37-39: 3 rows with col 3.
Rows 40-41: 2 rows with col 1.
Row 42: 1 row with col 2.
Rows 43-47: 5 rows with col 1.
Rows 48: 1 row with col 2. Place marker at each end of this row.
Rows 49-50: 2 rows with col 1.
Rows 50-53: 3 rows with col 3.
Rows 54-55: 2 rows with col 1.
Row 56: 1 row with col 2.
Rows 57-61: 5 rows with col 1.
Row 62: 1 row with col 3.
Rows 63-64: 2 rows with col 1.
Rows 65-67: 3 rows with col 2.
Rows 68-69: 2 rows with col 1.
Row 70: 1 row with col 3.
Rows 71-74: 4 rows with col 1.
Do not fasten off.

### Form and seam hood

Fold the top edge of the work in half with RS facing together, join together along top edge with dc to form hood.
Fasten off.

**Designed by**

## Donna Jones

Donna designs, edits and teaches yarn crafts. She believes creative expression is essential for our well-being and aims to instil this in others. Follow her on Instagram @djonesdesigns www.donnajonesdesigns.co.uk

Sew in all ends to WS of work

## Edging

With RS facing and using col 1, fasten on at the marker on the fold line.
Begin working in rounds as follows:
Rnd 1: ch 1, (placing marker or safety pin in first st) work 2 dc in each row edge of tr down left side edge, across hood, up along edge to corner, 3 dc in the corner st, 1 dc in each st along front top edge, 3 dc in the corner st, 2 dc in each row of tr up right side edge, and ss to first (marked) dc.
Remove marker.
Rnds 2-5: ch 1, 1 dc same place (replacing marker or safety pin in first st), 1 dc in each dc around edge, working 3 dc in each corner, join with ss in first (marked) dc.
Remove marker.
With RS facing, and front positioned over back ensuring edge of front lines up with markers placed at each end of Row 48 of back, place 5 markers evenly along the two front side edges to indicate placement of buttonholes.
Rnd 6 (Buttonholes): ch 1, 1 dc in same place (placing marker or safety pin in first st), 1 dc in each dc to 1 st before first marker, (3ch, skip 3 dc, 1 dc in each dc to 1 st before next marker) 4 times, 3ch, skip 3 dc, 1 dc in each dc to top corner of front, 3 dc in the corner st, 1 dc in each dc along front top edge, 3 dc in the corner st, (1 dc in each dc to 1 st before next marker, 3ch, skip 3 dc) 5 times, 1 dc in each dc to end, join with a ss in first (marked) dc. Remove all markers.
Rnd 7: ch 1, 1 dc in same place (replacing marker or safety pin in first st), 1 dc in each dc to first 3 ch-sp, (3 dc in 3 ch-sp, 1 dc in each dc to next 3 ch-sp) 4 times, 3 dc in next 3ch-sp, 1 dc in each dc to top corner of front, 3 dc in the corner st, 1 dc in each dc along front top edge, 3 dc in the corner st, (1 dc in each dc to next 3 ch-sp, 3 dc in ch-sp) 5 times, 1 dc in each dc to end, join with a ss in first (marked) dc.
Remove marker.
Rnds 8-10: ch 1, 1 dc in same place (placing marker or safety pin in first st), 1 dc in each dc along side edge of back, across hood, along second side edge of back to top corner of front, 3 dc in the corner st, 1 dc in each dc along front top edge, 3 dc in the corner st, 1 dc in each dc along side edge of front, join with a ss into first (marked) dc.
Remove marker.

## Reverse dc edging

Change to col 2.
Next Rnd: ch 1, 1 rdc in each dc around edge, working 3 rev dc in each of the 2 corners, join with a ss to first rdc.
Fasten off.

## Finishing

Sew in all remaining ends and spray block.
Sew buttons on back edging to correspond with buttonholes.

## Pattern notes

• This project is sized for a newborn baby. It is simple to adjust the size to suit larger babies as well. To adjust the width add sts to the foundation chain in multiples of 3; to adjust length add rows. Don't forget you will need more yarn to make a bigger sleeping bag.

• For baby's safety it is important to ensure the bag is not so large they can slip down too far as this can cause them to get overheated. As with any bedding, their face should remain above the cover which should tuck under their arms, and make sure they are placed with their feet are at the end of their crib, Moses basket, pram etc.

Designed by

# Sian Brown

After doing a Fashion/Textiles BA, Sian worked supplying machine knits to high street retailers. She became interested in handknits and has been designing them ever since, working for magazines, publishers and yarn companies. Her book Knitted Home is available now. www.sianbrown.co.uk

# Textured hot water bottle cosy

This pretty, striped hot water bottle cover will make an ideal gift. You could even work it in shades to match a room's decor

## Difficulty

★★★★☆

## What you need

- 5mm hook (US H/8)
- Yarn needle
- You will need Aran weight yarn in your chosen colours. We have used Debbie Bliss Cashmerino in:
  Colour 1: Mulberry (50g)
  Colour 2: Ecru (50g)

## Tension

17 stitches and 17 rows = 10 x 10cm (4 x 4in) over dc using 5mm hook. 8 stitches and 11 rows = 10 x 10cm (4 x 4in) over five stitch marguerite cluster pattern using 5mm hook.

## Measurements

22cm wide x 34cm long.

## Special stitches

Five stitch marguerite cluster (M5C): Pick up spike loops (by inserting hook and drawing yarn through) inserting hook as follows: into loop which closed previous M5C, under the two threads of last spike loop of previous M5C, into same place as last spike loop of previous M5C, and into next two sts – you now have six loops on hook. Hook yarn and draw yarn through all loops.

## Pattern notes

- The fabric made with the marguerite stitch pattern will have a tendency to lean towards the right. This is addressed by gently pulling and pinning the work straight during the blocking process.

## Pattern

### Side (make 2)

With 5mm hook and col 1 ch 38.

Foundation row (WS): 1 dc into 2nd ch from hook, 1 dc in every ch to end. (37 sts)

Row 1: ch 3, make 1 M5C by inserting hook into 2nd and 3rd chain from hook, and then into first 3 sts (to pick up the five spike loops), (1 ch, M5C) to last st, turn.

Row 2: ch 1, 1 dc into loop that closed last M5C, (1 dc in to next ch, 1 dc into loop that closed next M5C) across row, ending with 1 dc into each of next 2 ch, turn.

Change to col 2.

Rows 3 and 4: As rows 1 and 2.

These four rows set pattern and stripes. Cont in stripes until work measures 30cm (11¾in) ending with row 4 (col 2).

Cont in col 1 only.

Eyelet row (RS): ch 1, 1 dc in 1st dc, (ch 1, skip 1 dc, work 1 dc in next dc) rep to end, turn.

Next row: ch 1, work 1 dc in each dc and each ch gap to end, turn. (37 sts)

Next row: ch 1, dc to end.

Rep last row until work measures 33.5cm (13in).

Change to col 2 and work one more dc row.

Fasten off.

## Finishing

Weave in ends, pin the pieces to size and shape (see pattern notes). Join base and side seams.

Plait four strands of col 1 and four strands of col 2 together to form a cord and thread through eyelets.

# Spike stitch placemat and coaster

Utilise this interesting stitch for a stylish solution to protect your surfaces

## Difficulty

★★☆☆☆

## What you need

- 4mm hook (G/6)
- Yarn needle
- You will need to use DK weight yarn in your chosen colours. We have used Debbie Bliss Cotton DK in:
  Colour 1: Aqua (50g)
  Colour 2: Teal (50g)
  Colour 3: Avocado (100g)

## Tension

16 stitches and 20 rows = 10 x 10cm (4 x 4in) in double crochet.

## Measurements

Placemat: Width: 38cm (15in)
Depth: 32cm (12in)
Coaster: 10cm (4in)

## Special stitches

Spike stitch [SP]: Instead of working a dc into the top of the stitch of the previous row or round, work into the stitch on the row or round below. You can do various lengths of spike stitches. Spike stitches are also known as long and dropped stitches.

## Pattern

### Placemat

With col 1 and using 4mm (G/6) hook, make 60 ch.
Row 1 (WS): 1 dc into 2nd chain from hook, 1 dc into every ch to end, turn. (59 sts)
Rows 2 and 3: 1 ch, 1 dc into each st, turn.
Row 4 (RS, col 2): 1 ch, *1 dc into each of next 3 sts, 1 SP; rep from * to last 3 sts, 1 dc in last 3 sts, turn.
Rows 5-7 (col 3): As Row 2.
Row 8 (col 2): 1 ch, *1 dc into next 3 sts, 1 SP; rep from * to last 3 sts, 1 dc in last 3 sts, turn.
Rows 9-11 (col 1): Rep rows 5-7.
Repeat rows 4-11 until you have completed 63 rows.
Fasten off.

### Edging

With RS facing you, join col 2 to top-right corner, work 58 dc along top of placemat, 3 dc in corner, 48 dc evenly down side of mat, 3 dc in corner, 57 dc across bottom, 3 dc in corner, 48 dc up side of mat, work 2 dc in corner where edging started and join to first dc with sl st.
Fasten off and weave in ends.

### Coaster

With Col 1, ch 16.
Row 1 (WS): 1 dc into 2nd chain from hook, 1 dc into every ch to end, turn. (15 sts)
Rows 2-3: 1 ch, 1 dc into each dc to end, turn.
Row 4 (RS, col 2): 1 ch, *1 dc into each of next 3 dc, 1 SP; rep * to last 3 sts, 3 dc, turn.
Rows 5-7 (col 3): As row 2.
Row 8 (col 2): 1 ch, *1 dc into each of next 3 dc, 1 SP; rep * to last 3 sts, 3 dc, turn.
Rows 9-11 (col 1): As rows 5-7.
Repeat rows 4-11 once more.
Fasten off.

### Coaster edging

With RS facing, join col 2 to top-right corner, work 14 dc along top of coaster, 3 dc into corner, work 13 dc evenly down side of coaster, 3 dc in corner, 14 dc across bottom, 3 dc into corner, 13 dc up side of coaster, work 2 dc into corner where edging started and join to first dc with sl st. Fasten off.

### Finishing

Weave in all ends.

Designed by
**Sian Brown**

After doing a Fashion/Textiles BA, Sian worked supplying machine knits to high street retailers. She became interested in handknits and has been designing them ever since, working for magazines, publishers and yarn companies. Her book Knitted Home is available now. www.sianbrown.co.uk

# Linked stitches pincushion

Use up odd bits of yarn with this colourful and useful creation

## Difficulty

★★★☆☆

## What you need

- 3.5mm hook (US E/4)
- Small square of fabric 30 x 30cm (12 x 12in).
- Sewing needle and thread.
- You will need DK weight yarn in your chosen colours. We have used Rico Essentials Cotton in:
  Colour 1: Medium Blue, 34; oddments
  Colour 2: Lemon, 62; oddments
  Colour 3: Aquamarine, 31; oddments
  Colour 4: Magenta, 13; oddments
  Colour 5: Cobalt Blue, 32; oddments

## Measurements

Approx 13 x 13cm (5¼ x 5¼in).

Designed by
**Lynne Rowe**

Lynne Rowe is a freelance knit and crochet designer, technical editor, craft author and tutor. Lynne loves to pass on her skills to help others to knit, crochet and create. Read more about Lynne's yarn adventures at: www.thewoolnest.blogspot.co.uk and www.knitcrochetcreate.com

## Pattern

### Central linked rings link 1

Using 3.5mm (D/3) hook and col 1 make 14 ch, *join with a sl st in first ch to form a ring.

Rnd 1: ch 1 (not counted as a st), 24 dc into the ring, sl st to first dc to join. (24 sts)

Rnd 2: ch 1 (not counted as a st), 1 dc in each st around, sl st to first dc to join.

Cut yarn and fasten off.

### Link 2

Using col 2 make 14 ch, then threading the end of the ch from back to front through Link 1, join with a sl st in first ch.

Complete as for Link 1.

### Link 3

Using col 3 make 14 ch, then threading the end of the ch from back to front through Link 2, join with a sl st in first ch.

Complete as for Link 1.

### Link 4

Using col 4 make 14 ch, then threading the end of the ch from back to front through Link 3 and then from front back through Link 1, join with a sl st in first ch.

Complete as for Link 1.

### Square

Using col 5, join with a sl st to any dc of Link 1.

Rnd 1: ch 1 (not counted as a st), 1 dc in same st, 1 dc in each of next 3 sts, ch 2 (to make a corner), skip next st, 1 dc in each of next 4 sts, *ch 3, 1 dc in next 4 sts of next Link, ch 2 (corner made), skip next st, 1 dc in each of next 4 st; rep from * twice more, ch 3, sl st to first dc to join, fasten off.
(32 dc, 4 edged ch 3 sps,
4 corner ch 2 sps)

Change to col 3 and join with a sl st to any ch 2 corner sp.

Rnd 2 (col 3): ch 2 (counts as first htr), (1 htr, ch 2, 2 htr) into corner ch sp, *1 htr in each of next 4 sts, 1 htr into each of ch 3, 1 htr into each of next 4 sts, (2 htr, ch 2, 2 htr) in next corner sp; rep from * twice more, 1 htr in each of next 4 sts, 1 htr into each of ch 3, 1 htr into each of next 4 sts, sl st to top of beginning ch 2 to join, fasten off. (15 htr along each side, ch 2 in each corner)

Change to col 1 and join with a sl st to any corner sp.

Rnd 3 (col 1): ch 3 (counts as first tr), (2 tr, ch 2, 3 tr) into corner ch sp, *skip next st, 1 tr in each of next 14 sts**,
(3 tr, ch 2, 3 tr) in next corner sp; rep from * three times more, ending last rep at **, sl st to top of beginning ch 3 to join, fasten off. (20 tr along each side, ch 2 in each corner)

Change to col 4 and join with a sl st to any corner sp.

Rnd 4 (col 4): ch 3 (counts as first tr), (2 tr, ch 2, 3 tr) into corner ch sp, *1 tr in each of next 3 sts, (ch 1, skip next st, 1 tr in next st) 3 times, 1 tr in each of next 3 sts, (ch 1, skip next st, 1 tr in next st) 3 times, 1 tr in each of next 2 sts**,
(3 tr, ch 2, 3 tr) in next corner sp; rep from * twice more, then from * to **, sl st to top of beginning ch 3 to join, fasten off. (20 tr and ch 6 sps along each side, ch 2 in each corner)

### Edge

Change to col 2 and join with a sl st to any corner.

Next Rnd (col 2): *ch 2, skip next st, sl st in next st; rep from * to end.

Fasten off.

### Finishing

Cut 2 pieces of fabric 1cm (0.39in) larger than the linked square and place pieces with RS together. Keeping a 1cm (0.39in) seam allowance, sew 3 sides of the fabric using back stitch or by machine. Turn the right way out and fill with toy filling. Sew the remaining seam closed using small stitches. Place the linked square on top of the cushion and sew in place using small stitches.

# Traditional tea cosy

Test your skills and add some retro charm to a teapot

## Difficulty

★★★☆☆

## What you need

- 4 mm hook (US G/6)
- 4.5 mm hook (US G/7)
- Yarn needle
- You will need to use Aran weight yarn in your chosen colours. We have used Drops Nepal yarn in:
  Colour 1: Off-white (50g)
  Colour 2: Orange Mix (50g)
  Colour 3: Cerise (50g)
  Colour 4: Light Olive (50g)
  Colour 5: Light Grey Green (50g)

## Tension

16 stitches and 8.5 rows = 10 x 10cm (4 x 4in) over main pattern using 4.50mm (7) hook.

## Measurements

Width: 21.5cm (8.4 in) Depth: 18cm (7.08in) (excluding gathered top)

## Designed by Sian Brown

After doing a Fashion/Textiles BA, Sian worked supplying machine knits to high street retailers. She became interested in handknits and has been designing them ever since, working for magazines, publishers and yarn companies. Her book Knitted Home is available now. www.sianbrown.co.uk

## Pattern

### Tea cosy sides (make 2)

Using 4mm (G/6) hook and col 1 make 36 ch.

Row 1 (RS): 1 dc into 2nd ch from hook, 1 dc into each ch to end, turn. (35 sts)

Row 2: ch 1, 1 dc into each dc to end, turn.

With RS facing work the following:

### Colour sequence

1 row of each colour in the following order: col 2, col 3, col 4, col 1 and col 5.

Change to col 2 and 4.5mm (7) crochet hook.

Foundation Row (RS, col 2): ch 4 (count as first tr and ch 1 sp), skip 2 dc, * 3 tr into next dc, ch 1, skip 3 dc; rep from * to last 4 sts, 3 tr into next dc, skip 2 dc, 1 tr into dc, fasten off, DO NOT TURN.

Change to col 3.

Row 1 (RS, col 3): Join with sl st into 3rd ch at beg of prev row, ch 3 (count as first tr), 2 tr into first ch sp, * ch 1, 3 tr into next ch sp; rep from * to last 3 tr and ch sp, ch 1, skip 3 tr, 2 tr into last ch sp, 1 tr into last tr, fasten off. DO NOT TURN.

Change to col 4.

Row 2 (RS, col 4): Join with sl st into 3rd ch at beg of prev row, ch 4 (count as first tr and ch 1 sp), skip 2 tr, * 3 tr into next ch sp, ch 1; rep from * to last 3 tr, skip 2 tr, 1 tr into last tr, fasten off.

DO NOT TURN.

These last 2 rows set the pattern ONLY. Rep these 2 rows 5 times more, AT SAME TIME rep the colour sequence as stated above, thus ending with a patt row 2 with col 4.

### Top edge with eyelets

Change to 4mm (G/6) hook.

With RS facing and using col 1 only, join with sl st into 3rd ch at beg of prev row.

Next Row: ch 1, dc into same place, 1 dc into each ch sp and tr of previous row, turn. (35 sts)

Next Row: ch1, 1 dc into each dc to end, turn.

Eyelet Row (RS): ch 1, 1 dc into first dc, * ch1, skip next dc, 1 dc into each of next 3 dc; rep from * 7 times more, ch 1, skip next dc, 1 dc into last dc of row, turn.

Next Row: ch 1, 1 dc into each dc and ch sp, turn. (35 sts)

Next Row: ch 1, 1 dc into each dc to end, turn.

Rep last row 3 times more.

Fasten off.

### Crochet flowers (make 2)

Using 4mm (G/6) crochet hook and col 3, make a magic ring and ch 1.

Rnd 1: 10 dc into ring, pull the ring closed, sl st into first dc of rnd.

Rnd 2: * ch 3, 2 tr into back loop only of next dc and leaving the last loop of each on hook, yo and draw through all loops on hook, ch 3, sl st into next dc, (petal made), rep from * to end, working last sl st into base of first ch 3 of round (total 5 petals made).

Fasten off.

### Picot edging

First, sew up sides of tea cosy leaving space open for spout and handle.

With RS facing and using 4mm (G/6) hook with col 2, join with a sl st into dc of previous row at either top side seam.

Picot Row: 1 dc into same place as sl st, 1 dc into next dc, * ch 3, sl st into 3rd ch from hook (picot made),1 dc into each of next 3 dc; rep from * to last 2 dc, ch 3, sl st into 3rd ch from hook, 1 dc into each of last 2 dc, sl st into first dc of rnd.

Fasten off.

### Finishing

Using 4mm (G/6) crochet hook and col 5 make chain 60cm long for the drawstring. Thread crochet cord through the eyelets, beginning and ending at the centre of the side of the cosy. Sew 1 flower to each end of cord using the yarn left at the ends. Pull cord tight to fit your teapot.

# Embellished bunting

Take bunting to the next level by creating some pretty flower embellishments

## Difficulty

★★★☆☆

## What you need

- 4mm hook (US G/6)
- Yarn needle
- You will need to use DK weight yarn, in your chosen colours. Here we have used Rowan Pure Wool DK in:
  Colour 1: Pink (50g)
  Colour 2: Teal (50g)
  Colour 3: Lime (50g)
  Colour 4: White (50g)

## Measurements

Total length: 257.5cm (101.3in). Each granny triangle measures 17.5cm (6.8in) along top edge with a depth of 15.5cm (6.1in)

## Designed by Donna Jones

Donna designs, edits and teaches yarn crafts. She believes creative expression is essential for our well-being and aims to instil this in others. Follow her on Instagram @djonesdesigns www.donnajonesdesigns.co.uk

## Pattern

### Granny triangles (make 3 in colours 1, 2 and 3)

Using 4mm (G/6) hook, ch 4 and join with sl st to form a ring.

Rnd 1: 3 ch (counts as 1 tr), 3 tr in ring, 2 ch, [4 tr in ring, 2 ch] twice, join with sl st into 3rd of 3 ch from beginning of round.

Rnd 2: Sl st in next 3 tr and into 1st ch sp, 3 ch (counts as 1 tr), (3 tr, 2 ch, 4 tr) in same sp, [1 ch, (4 tr, 2 ch, 4 tr) all in next sp] twice, 1 ch join with sl st in 3rd of 3 ch from beginning of round.

Rnd 3: Sl st in next 3 tr and in next 2-ch sp, 3 ch (counts as 1 tr), (3 tr, 2 ch, 4 tr) in same sp, 1 ch, [3 tr in next 1-ch sp, 1 ch, (4 tr, 2 ch, 4tr,) in next 2-ch sp, 1 ch] twice, 3 tr into next 2-ch sp, 1 ch, join with sl st in 3rd of 3 ch from beg of round.

Note: After this point it will be clear to the maker which spaces are corners and which are at the edges.

Rnd 4: Sl st in next 3 tr and in next corner ch sp, 3 ch (counts as 1 tr), (3 tr, 2 ch, 4 tr) in same sp, 1 ch, *[3 tr in next edge ch sp, 1 ch] twice, (4 tr, 2 ch, 4 tr) in next corner ch sp, 1 ch, rep from * once more, [3 tr in next edge ch sp, 1 ch] twice, join with sl st to 3rd of 3 ch from beginning of round.

Rnd 5: Sl st in next 3 tr and in next corner ch sp, 3 ch (counts as 1 tr), (3 tr, 2 ch, 4 tr) in same sp, 1 ch, *[3 tr into next edge ch sp, 1 ch] 3 times, (4 tr, 2 ch, 4tr) in next corner ch sp, 1 ch; rep from * once more, [3 tr in next edge ch sp, 1 ch] 3 times, join with sl st to 3rd of 3 ch from beginning of round.

Rnd 6: Sl st in next 3 tr and in next corner 2 ch sp, 3 ch (counts as 1 tr), (3 tr, 2 ch, 4 tr) in same sp, 1 ch, *[3 tr in next edge ch sp, 1 ch] 4 times, (4 tr, 2 ch, 4tr) in next corner ch sp, 1 ch; rep from * once more, [3 tr into next edge ch sp, 1 ch] 4 times, join with sl st to 3rd of 3 ch from beginning of round.

Rnd 7: ch 1 (does not count as a st), 1 dc in st at base of ch, 1 dc in each next 3 tr, 5 dc in corner ch sp, 1 dc in each next 4 tr, *[1dc in next edge ch sp, 1 dc in each next 3tr] 4 times, 1 dc in next edge ch sp, 1 dc in each next 4 tr, 5 dc in corner ch sp, 1 dc in each next 4 tr, rep from * once more, [1 dc in next edge ch sp, 1 dc in each next 3 tr] 4 times, 1 dc in next edge ch sp, sl st to 1st dc from beginning of round.

Rnd 8: ch 1 (does not count as st), 1 dc into st at base of ch, 1 dc in each next 5 dc, 3dc in next dc, [1 dc in each next 29 dc, 3 dc in next dc] twice, 1 dc into each next 23 dc, sl st to first dc from beginning of round. Fasten off.

### Large layered flower (make 5)

Using col 4, make a magic ring and ch 1.

Rnd 1: 6 dc into ring. Pull the ring closed.

Rnd 2: [ch 2, 1 tr in front loop of next dc, 2 ch, sl st in front loop of same dc] 6 times. (6 petals made)

Rnd 3: [ch 1, 1 tr into back loop of next tr on prev row] 6 times, sl st into 1 ch sp from beginning of round.

Rnd 4: ch 2, 2 tr into ch sp at base of ch, 2 ch, sl st in same ch sp, [2 ch, 2 tr in next ch sp, 2 ch, sl st into same ch sp] 5 times. (6 petals made)

Fasten off.

### Medium flower (make 4)

Using col 4, make a magic ring and ch 1

Rnd 1: [1 dc into ring, 1 ch] 6 times, pull magic ring closed and join with sl st to dc from beginning of round.

Rnd 2: [Sl st in next ch sp, (2 ch, 2 tr, 2 ch, sl st) all in same sp]
6 times. (6 petals made)
Fasten off.

### Small flower (make 5)

Using col 4, make a magic ring and ch 1.

Rnd 1: [ch 7, 1 dc into ring]
6 times. (6 petals made).
Fasten off.

### Medium rose (make 5)

Using col 4, ch 18.

Row 1: 1 tr into 4th ch from hook, 2 tr into every ch to end.

Fasten off.

Gently position the coil into a rose shape

and stitch in place at the back.

### Small rose (make 5)

Make ch 15.

Row 1: 1 dc into 3rd ch from hook, 2 dc into each ch to end.

Fasten off.

Gently position the coil into a rose shape and stitch in place at the back.

### Finishing

Darn in any ends and block all triangles to ensure they lay flat.

Arrange triangles in the order in which you would like them to appear. To join, you will make a cord and crochet over the top of each flag, thus:

Joining Row: Using 4mm (G/6) hook and colour 1, ch 30, then with RS facing and beginning at the top-right corner, work 1 dc into each st across the top of the first triangle and ch 10 before working across next triangle as before. Continue joining triangles in this way, with 10 ch between each triangle until last one is completed, work 30 ch and turn.

Next Row: Sl st into every st to end.

Fasten off.

Sew in the ends of the cord. Sew in spare ends of flowers before stitching in place to bunting as required.

### Pattern notes

- For a slightly easier project, omit the flowers.

# Perky peg bag

Hang out your washing in style with this fun peg bag design

## Difficulty

★★☆☆☆

## What you need

- 4mm hook (G/6)
- Yarn needle
- 21cm (8.2in wooden hanger with unscrewable cup hook or wood dowel and screw-in hook.
- You will need DK weight yarn in your chosen colours. We have used Rowan Handknit Cotton DK in:
  Colour 1: Aqua, 327; (100g)
  Colour 2: Sugar, 303; (50g).
  Colour 3: Celery, 309; (50g)

## Tension

17 sts and 21 rows = 10 x 10cm (4 x 4in) over double crochet stitch using 4mm (G/6) hook

## Measurements

Widest point: 30cm (11.81in) Length: 30cm (11.81in)

Designed by
**Donna Jones**

Donna designs, edits and teaches yarn crafts. She believes creative expression is essential for our well-being and aims to instil this in others. Follow her on Instagram @djonesdesigns www.donnajonesdesigns.co.uk

## Pattern

### Back

*Using 4mm (US G/6) hook and col 1, ch 47.

Row 1 (RS): 1 dc into 2nd ch from hook (counts as 1 dc), 1 dc into next and each ch to end, turn. (46 sts)

Row 2 (inc): ch 1 (does not count as a st), 1 dc into next dc, 2 dc into next dc, 1 dc into each dc to last 2 sts, 2 dc into next dc, 1 dc, turn. (48 sts)*

Row 3: ch 1 (does not count as a st), 1 dc into each dc to end, turn.

Row 4 (inc): Repeat row 2 for 1 row (50 sts)

Rows 5-10: Rep row 3. (6 rows of 50 sts)

Row 11 (dec): ch 1 (does not count as a st), dc2tog over next 2 sts, 1 dc into each dc to last 3 sts, dc2tog over next 2 sts, 1 dc in next dc, turn. (48 sts)

Row 12-16: Rep row 3. (5 rows of 48 sts)

Change to col 2

Rows 17-18: Rep row 3. (2 rows of 48 sts)

Fasten off col 2. Change to col 1.

Rows 19-21: Rep row 3. (3 rows of 48 sts)

Row 22 (dec): ch 1 (does not count as a st), dc2tog over next 2 sts, 1 dc into each dc to last 3 sts, dc2tog over next 2 sts, 1 dc in next dc, turn. (46 sts)

Rows 23-32: Rep row 3. (10 rows of 46 sts)

Row 33 (dec): ch 1 (does not count as a st), dc2tog over next 2 sts, 1 dc into each dc to last 3 sts, dc2tog over next 2 sts, 1 dc in next dc, turn. (44 sts)

Rows 34: Rep row 3. (44 sts)

Change to col 3.

Rows 35-36: Repeat row 3 (2 rows of 44 sts)

Fasten off col 3. Change to col 1.

Rows 37-43: Rep row 3. (7 rows of 44 sts)

Row 44 (dec): ch 1 (does not count as a st), dc2tog over next 2 sts, 1 dc into each dc to last 3 sts, dc2tog over next 2 sts, 1 dc in next dc, turn. (42 sts)

Rows 45-52: Rep row 3. (8 rows of 42 sts)

Change to col 2.

Rows 53-54: Rep row 3 (2 rows of 42 sts)

Fasten off col 2.

Change to col 1.

Row 55 (dec): ch 1 (does not count as a st), dc2tog over next 2 sts, 1 dc into each dc to last 3 sts, dc2tog over next 2 sts, 1 dc in last dc, turn. (40sts)

Rows 56-60: Rep row 3 (5 rows of 40 sts)

Fasten off.

### Front

Work as given for back from * to *.

Join in col 2 and continue as follows:

Row 3 (RS): ch 1 (does not count as a st), 1 dc into each dc to end, turn.

Row 4 (inc): ch 1 (does not count as a st), 1 dc into next dc, 2 dc into next dc, 1 dc into each dc to last 2 sts, 2 dc into next dc, 1 dc in next dc, turn. (50 sts)

Rows 5-8: Repeat row 3 (4 rows of 50 sts)

Change to col 3.

Rows 9-10: Rep row 3 (2 rows of 50 sts)

Change to col 1.

Row 11 (dec): ch 1 (does not count as a st), dc2tog over next 2 sts, 1 dc into each dc to last 3 sts, dc2tog, 1 dc in next dc, turn. (48 sts)

Rows 12-16: Rep row 3 (5 rows of 48 sts)

Change to col 2.

Rows 17-18: Rep row 3 (2 rows of 48 sts)

Change to col 3.

Rows 19-21: Rep row 3 (3 rows of 48 sts)

Row 22 (dec): 1 ch (does not count as a st), dc2tog over next 2 sts, 1 dc into each dc to last 3 sts, dc2tog over next 2 sts, 1 dc in next dc, turn. (46 sts)

Rows 23-26: Rep row 3. (4 rows of 46 sts)

Change to col 1.

Rows 27-28: Rep row 3 (2 rows of 46 sts)

Change to col 2.

Rows 29-32: Rep row 3 (4 rows of 46 sts)

Row 33 (dec): ch 1 (does not count as a st), dc2tog over next 2 sts, 1 dc into each dc to last 3 sts, dc2tog over next 2 sts, 1 dc in next dc, turn. (44 sts)

## Pattern notes

- There is no need to cut off a colour while you are working, as when working even numbers of rows, you will always return to the end where your other colours are sitting. Simply carry them up the side of your work and catch in as necessary.

**Row 34:** Rep row 3. (44 sts)
Change to col 3.
**Rows 35-36:** Rep row 3 (2 rows of 44 sts)
Change to col 1.
**Rows 37-40:** Rep row 3 (4 rows of 44 sts)

## Divide for opening

**Row 41 (RS):** Using col 2, ch 1 (does not count as a st), 1 dc into each next 11 dc, turn. (11 sts)
**Row 42:** Rep row 3. (11 sts)
Change to col 3.
**Row 43 (inc):** ch 1 (does not count as a st), 1 dc into each next 9 dc, 2 dc into next dc, 1 dc into next dc, turn. (12 sts)
**Row 44 (dec):** ch 1 (does not count as a st), 1 dc into each next 9 dc, dc2tog over next 2 sts, 1 dc into next dc, turn. (11 sts)
**Row 45 (inc):** ch 1 (does not count as a st), 1 dc into each next 9 dc, 2 dc into next dc, 1 dc into next dc, turn. (12 sts)
**Row 46:** Rep row 3. (12 sts)
**Row 47 (inc):** ch 1 (does not count as a st), 1 dc into each next 10 dc, 2 dc into next dc, 1 dc into next dc, turn. (13 sts)
**Row 48 (inc):** ch 1 (does not count as a st), 1 dc into next dc, 2 dc into next dc, 1 dc into each dc to end, turn. (14 sts)
**Row 49 (inc):** ch 1(does not count as a st), 1 dc into each next 12 dc, 2 dc into next dc, 1 dc in next dc, turn. (15 sts)
Fasten off.

It's now time to work the other side of the opening.
**Row 41:** With RS facing, miss centre 22 sts and using col 2, rejoin yarn with 1 dc, work 1 dc into each next 10 dc, turn. (11 sts)
**Row 42:** Rep row 3. (11 sts)
Join in col 3.
**Row 43 (inc):** ch 1 (does not count as a st), 1 dc into next dc, 2 dc into next dc, 1 dc into each dc to end, turn. (12 sts)
**Row 44 (dec):** ch 1 (does not count as a st), 1 dc into next dc, dc2tog over next 2 sts, 1 dc into each dc to end, turn. (11 sts)
**Row 45 (inc):** ch 1 (does not count as a st), 1 dc into next dc, 2 dc into next dc, 1dc into each dc to end. (12 sts)
**Row 46:** Rep row 3. (12 sts)
**Row 47 (inc):** ch 1 (does not count as a st), 1 dc into next dc, 2 dc into next dc, 1 dc into each dc to end, turn. (13 sts)
**Row 48 (inc):** ch 1 (does not count as a st), 1 dc into each next 12 dc, 2 dc into next dc, 1dc in next dc, turn. (14 sts)
**Row 49 (inc):** ch 1 (does not count as a st), 1 dc into next dc, 2 dc into next dc, 1 dc into each dc to end, turn. (15 sts)

## Rejoin opening

**Row 50 (WS):** ch 1 (does not count as a st), 1 dc into each of next 14 dc, 2 dc into next dc, ch 10, 2 dc into first dc across gap, 1 dc into each dc to end, turn.
Join in col 1.
**Row 51:** Using col 1, ch 1 (does not count as a st), 1 dc into each of next 16 dc, 1 dc into each of next 10 ch, 1 dc in each dc to end, turn. (42 sts)
**Row 52:** Rep row 3.
Fasten off col 1 and join in col 2.
**Row 53-54:** Rep row 3. (2 rows of 42 sts)
**Row 55 (dec):** ch 1 (does not count as a st), dc2tog over next 2 sts, 1 dc into each dc to last 3 sts, dc2tog, 1 dc in next dc, turn. (40 sts)
**Row 56:** Rep row 3. (40 sts) Change to col 3.
**Row 57-60:** Rep row 3.
(4 rows of 40 sts)
Fasten off.

## Finishing

Weave in ends and block lightly according to instructions on ball band.

## Front opening edging

With RS facing, using col 2, join yarn to bottom-left corner of opening, work 1 dc into each dc to corner, 3 dc into in corner sp, work 1 dc into each row edge or dc all around opening, 3 dc into each corner, join with ss to first dc and fasten off.

## Join Front and Back

With front and back held together with wrong sides facing, join yarn through both layers at bottom-right corner.
Working 1 dc for each row through both layers, join side edge together, working 3 dc into at top corner row end.
Work 1 dc through each of first 18 dc, work into back only for next 4 dc (for hook opening).
Resume working through both layers, work dc into each dc to corner, 3 dc into corner, 1 dc into each row end along side to bottom left corner, 3 dc into corner, 1 dc in each dc across bottom edge to end, working 3 dc into final corner, join with ss to first dc.
Fasten off and weave in ends.

Screw cup hook into centre of wood strip to make a hanger. Insert hanger into peg bag through front opening, position hook to come out at small opening at top edge.

# Aran cushion cover

It is possible to get the knitted aran look with a crochet hook. This cushion would look great teamed up with a fluffy throw

## Difficulty

★★★★☆

## What you need

- 4.5mm hook (US G/7)
- 50 x 50cm (20 x 20in) cushion pad
- Locking stitch markers or safety pins
- Yarn needle
- 5 x 2.5cm (1in) buttons
- Sewing needle and matching thread
- You will need Worsted weight wool in your chosen colour. We have used Sublime Extra Fine Merino Worsted in: Colour 1: Salty Grey, 010; 13 balls (650g)

## Measurements

Assembled cushion measures 50 x 50cm (30 x 30in).

## Designed by Donna Jones

Donna designs, edits and teaches yarn crafts. She believes creative expression is essential for our well-being and aims to instil this in others. Follow her on Instagram @djonesdesigns www.donnajonesdesigns.co.uk

## Pattern

### Front

Note: For all special stitches, see p76.

Using 4.5mm hook, ch 87.

Foundation Row: 1 tr into 4th ch from hook (counts as 3 ch and 1 tr), 1 tr into each ch to end, turn. (85 sts)

Row 1 (RS): 3 ch (counts as 1 tr), 1 tr into each of next 4 tr, C2F, 1 tr into each of next 3 tr, (C6F, 1 tr into each of next 3 tr) twice, C2F, 1 tr into each of next 4 tr, MB, 1 tr into each of next 5 tr, MB, 1 tr into each of next 3 tr, MB, 1 tr into each of next 5 tr, MB, 1 tr into each of next 4 tr, C2F, (1 tr into each of next 3 tr, C6F) twice, 1 tr into each of next 3 tr, C2F, 1 tr into each of next 4 tr, 1 tr in third ch of turning ch, turn.

Row 2 (WS): 3 ch (counts as 1 tr), 1 tr into each of next 4 tr, 1 BPdtr into each of next 2 dtr, 1 tr into each of next 3 tr, (1 BPdtr into each of next 6 dtr, 1 tr into each of next 3 tr) twice, 1 BPdtr into each of next 2 dtr, 1 tr into each of next 25 sts (i.e in tr or the top of bobbles made on previous row), 1 BPdtr into each of next 2 dtr, (1 tr into each of next 3 tr, 1 BPdtr into each of next 6 dtr) twice, 1 tr into each of next 3 tr, 1 BPdtr into each of next 2 dtr, 1 tr into each of next 4 tr, 1 tr in 3rd ch of 3 turning chain, turn.

Row 3: 3 ch (counts as 1 tr), 1 tr into each of next 4 tr, C2F, 1 tr into each of next 3 tr, (C6F, 1 tr into each of next 3 tr) twice, C2F, 1 tr into each of next 4 tr, MB, (1 tr into each of next 7 tr, MB) twice, 1 tr into each of next 4 tr, C2F, (1 tr into each of next 3 tr, C6F) twice, 1 tr into each of next 3 tr, C2F, 1 tr into each of next 4 tr, 1 tr in third ch of turning ch, turn.

Row 4: Rep Row 2.

Row 5: 3 ch (counts as 1 tr), 1 tr into each of next 4 tr, C2F, 1 tr into each of next 3 tr, (C6F, 1 tr into each of next 3 tr) twice, C2F, 1 tr into each of next 4 tr, MB, 1 tr into each of next 15 tr, MB, 1 tr into each of next 4 tr, C2F, (1 tr into each of next 3 tr, C6F) twice, 1 tr into each of next 3 tr, C2F, 1 tr into each of next 4 tr, 1 tr in third ch of turning ch, turn.

Row 6: Rep Row 2.

Row 7: Rep Row 3.

Row 8: Rep Row 2.

Row 9: Rep Row 1.

Row 10: Rep Row 2.

Row 11: 3 ch (counts as 1 tr), 1 tr into each of next 4 tr, C2F, 1 tr into each of next 3 tr, (C6F, 1 tr into each of next 3 tr) twice, C2F, 1 tr into each of next 4 tr, MB, (1 tr into each of next 3 tr, MB) 4 times, 1 tr into each of next 4 tr, C2F, (1 tr into each of next 3 tr, C6F) twice, 1 tr into each of next 3 tr, C2F, 1 tr into each of next 4 tr, 1 tr in third ch of turning ch, turn.

Row 12: Rep Row 2.

Rep Rows 1-12 twice more, and then Rows 1-10 once more, working a total of 47 rows, ending with Row 10.

Fasten off.

### Lower back panel

Using 4.5mm hook, make 96 ch.

Foundation Row: 1 tr in 4th ch from hook (counts as 3 ch and 1 tr), 1 tr into each ch to end, turn. (94 sts)

Row 1 (RS): 2 ch (counts as 1 htr), *1 FPtr into each of next 4 sts, 1 BPtr into each of next 4 sts; rep for * to last 5 sts, 1 FPtr into each of next 4 sts, 1 tr in top of turning ch, turn.

Row 2 (WS): 2 ch (counts as 1 htr), *1 BPtr into each of next 4 sts, 1 FPtr into each of next 4 sts; rep for * to last 5 sts, 1 BPtr into each of next 4 sts, 1 tr in top of turning ch, turn.

Row 3: Rep Row 1.

Row 4-5: Rep Row 2.

Row 6: Rep Row 1.

Row 7: Rep Row 2.

Row 8: Rep Row 1.

Rows 1-8 form Basket Weave Pattern.

Rep Rows 1-8 a further 5 times, and then rep Rows 1-4 once.

Fasten off.

### Upper back panel

Using 4.5mm hook, ch 83.

Row 1 (RS): 1 dc in 2nd ch from hook, 1 dc into each ch to end, turn. (82 sts)

Row 2: 1 ch (does not count as dc), 1 dc into each st to end, turn.

## Special stitches

C2F: Cross 2 stitches at the front: Skip 1 st, work 1 dtr in front post of next stitch, then work 1 dtr in front post of skipped stitch.
C6F: Cross 6 stitches at the front: Skip 3 stitches, work 1 dtr in front post of each of next 3 stitches, then work 1 dtr in front post of each of 3 skipped stitches beginning with the first skipped stitch.
MB: Work 5 dtr in next stitch, only working each stitch until 1 loop remains for each dtr (6 loops now on the hook), yarn over hook and pull through the 6 loops to form bobble.
Front post treble crochet (FPtr): Yarn over, insert the hook from front to back then to the front around the post of the next stitch, yarn over and draw up a loop, (yarn over and draw through two loops) twice.
Back post treble crochet (BPtr): Yarn over, insert the hook from back to front then to the back around the post of the next stitch, yarn over and draw up a loop, (yarn over and draw through two loops) twice.

## Pattern notes

- For a firmer edge to the upper back panel, work into the middle loop (or bump) on the back of the chain when working the foundation row.
- Stitch counts remain consistent throughout.

Rows 3-6: Rep Row 2 a further 4 times.
Row 7 (Buttonholes): 1 ch (does not count as st), 1 dc into each of next 7 dc, (4 ch, skip next 4 sts, 1 dc into each of next 12 dc) 4 times, 4 ch, skip next 4 sts, 1 dc into each of next 7 dc, turn. (5 buttonholes made)
Row 8: 1 ch (does not count as dc), 1 dc into each of next 7 dc, (4 dc into 4 ch sp, 1 dc into each of next 12 dc) 4 times, 4 dc into 4 ch sp, 1 dc into each of next 7 dc, turn.
Row 9-12: Rep Row 2
Row 13: 3 ch (counts as first 1 tr), 1 tr into each tr to end, turn.
Row 14-24: Rep Row 13.
Fasten off.

## Finishing

Weave in ends, pin out to size and spray block.
Place a marker at each side of Front, approx 19cm from the top edge. Place a marker at each side of Lower Back panel, approx 7cm from the top edge.
With RS facing upwards, lay Front panel flat. Place Upper panel on top of this with WS facing up, ensuring the top edge lines up with the top edge of the front. Now lay the bottom panel on top of both pieces with WS facing up, bottom edge lined up with bottom of from panel, and markers aligned with the markers on the front and upper back – there should be some overlap of the Upper and Lower Back panels. Secure in position with safety pins all around the edge. Sew all around the top, bottom and sides with backstitch.
Turn right side out through the opening on the back. Stitch buttons on Lower Back panel to align with buttonholes.
Place cushion insert inside and fasten with buttons for the final touch.

# Spiked cushion

Spruce up your couch with a funky spike cushion that's super quick and easy to make

## Difficulty

## What you need

- 10mm hook (US N,P/15)
- Cushion insert 38cm x 38cm
- You will need to use Super Chunky weight yarn in your chosen colours.
  Colour 1: Dark blue (50g)
  Colour 2: Mid blue (50g)
  Colour 3: Light blue (60g
  Colour 4: White (60g)

## Measurements

40.5cm x 40.5cm.

## Special stitches

Spike stitch [SP]: Instead of working a dc into the top of the stitch of the previous row or round, work into the stitch on the row or round below. You can do various lengths of spike stitches.
Standing dc: With slipknot already on hook, insert hook into stitch, yo & draw up a loop, then yo and pull through both loops on hook.

## Pattern notes

- When working spike stitches, pull up a generous loop to avoid the square pulling in towards the centre on the edges.

Designed by
**Shelley Husband**

Shelley is a long time crafter whose passion is designing crochet patterns. She lives with her husband and teenage daughters in a tiny town on the coast of Victoria, Australia.
www.spincushions.com

## Pattern

### Square (make 2)

Using 10mm hook in col 1, make a magic ring (alternatively ch 4, and join with ss to form a ring).
Rnd 1: ch 3 (counts as 1 tr), 11 tr into ring, join with ss to 3rd ch of ch 3. (12 sts)
Rnd 2: ch 3 (counts as 1 tr), 2 tr into base of 3 ch, *skip 2 sts**, (3 tr, ch 2, 3 tr) into next st; rep from * twice and from * to ** once, 3 tr in same place as first sts, ch 2, join with ss to 3rd ch of 3 ch. (6 sts along each side and 4 corner ch-2 sps)
Fasten off yarn and weave in ends.
Rnd 3: Join col 2 with a standing dc to any corner ch-2 sp,* dc in next 2 sts, spike dc in next 2 sts of Rnd 1 below, dc in next 2 sts**, (dc, ch 2, dc) into next corner ch-2 sp; rep from * twice and from * to ** once, dc in same sp as first st, ch 1, join with dc to standing dc. (8 sts along each side and 4 corner ch-2 sps)
Rnd 4: ch 3 (counts as 1 tr), tr over joining dc, *tr in next 8 sts**, (2 tr, ch 2, 2 tr) into next corner ch-2 sp; rep from * twice and from * to ** once, 2 tr in same sp as first sts, ch 2, join with ss to 3rd ch of 3 ch. (12 sts along each side and 4 corner ch-2 sps)
Fasten off yarn and weave in ends.
Rnd 5: Join col 3 with a standing dc to any corner ch-2 sp, *dc in next 5 sts, spike dc in next 2 sts of Rnd 3 below, dc in next 5 sts**, (dc, ch 2, dc) into next corner ch-2 sp; rep from * twice and from * to ** once, dc in same sp as first st, ch 1, join with dc to standing dc. (14 sts along each side and 4 corner ch-2 sps)
Rnd 6: ch 3 (counts as 1 tr), *tr in next 14 sts**, (tr, ch 2, tr) into next corner ch-2 sp; rep from * twice and from * to ** once, tr in same sp as first st, ch 2, join with ss to 3rd ch of 3 ch. (16 sts along each side and 4 corner ch-2 sps)
Fasten off yarn and weave in ends.
Rnd 7: Join col 4 with a standing dc to any corner ch-2 sp, *dc in next 7 sts, spike dc in next 2 sts of Rnd 5 below, dc in next 7 sts**, (dc, ch 2, dc) into next corner ch-2 sp; rep from * twice and from * to ** once, dc in same sp as first st, ch 1, join with dc to standing dc. (18 sts along each side and 4 corner ch-2 sps)
Rnd 8: ch 3 (counts as 1 tr), *tr in next 18 sts**, (tr, ch 2, tr) into next corner ch-2 sp; rep from * twice and from * to ** once, tr in same sp as first st, ch 1, join with dc to 3rd ch of 3 ch. (20 sts along each side and 4 corner ch-2 sps)
Rnd 9: ch 3 (counts as 1 tr), tr over joining dc, *tr in next 20 sts**, (2 tr, ch 2, 2 tr) into next corner ch-2 sp; rep from * twice and from * to ** once, 2 tr in same sp as first st, ch 2, join with ss to 3rd ch of 3 ch. (24 sts along each side and 4 corner ch-2 sps)
Fasten off yarn and weave in ends.

## Finishing

Hold squares wrong sides together. Join col 4 with a standing dc through the corner ch-2 sps of both squares, dc in same corner ch-2 sps, *dc in next 24 sts of both squares at the same time**, 3 dc into next corner ch-2 sps of both squares; rep from * twice, insert cushions insert and rep from * to ** once, dc in same sp as first sts, join with ss to standing dc. Fasten off yarn and weave in ends.

# Teddy bear

Create a companion in the form of a teddy bear with this quick and easy project that would make a perfect baby gift!

### Difficulty
★★☆☆☆

### What you need
- 3.75mm hook (US F/5)
- 1 pair 6mm safety eyes
- Yarn needle
- Fiberfill stuffing
- Brown yarn for face
- You will need to use DK weight yarn in your chosen colours. We have used Bernat Handicrafter cotton.
  Colour 1: Skin (1 ball)

### Measurements
23cm tall.

## Pattern

### Head
Using 3.75 mm hook, make a magic ring.
Rnd 1: 6 dc into ring and pull it closed. (6 sts)
Rnd 2: 2 dc in each dc. (12 sts)
Rnd 3: (1 dc in next dc, 2 dc in next dc) 6 times. (18 sts)
Rnd 4: 1 dc in each dc. (18 sts)
Rnd 5: (1 dc in each of next 2 dc, 2 dc in next dc) 6 times. (24 sts)
Rnd 6: (1 dc in each of next 3 dc, 2 dc in next dc) 6 times. (30 sts)
Rnd 7: (1 dc in each of next 4 dc, 2 dc in next dc) 6 times. (36 sts)
Rnds 8-11: 1 dc in each dc. (4 rnds of 36 sts)
Rnd 12: (1 dc in each of next 4 dc, dc2tog in next 2 dc) 6 times. (30 sts)
Rnd 13: (1 dc in each of next 3 dc, dc2tog in next 2 dc) 6 times. (24 sts)
Rnd 14: (1 dc in each of next 2 dc, dc2tog in next 2 dc) 6 times. (18 sts)

### Assemble the face
Insert 6 mm safety eyes between rnd 1 and rnd 2 of the head and position them 4 sts apart from each other.
Embroider a nose and mouth between the eyes on the magic loop and rnd 1 using a yarn needle and brown yarn.
Stuff the head firmly.

Rnd 15: (1 dc in next dc, dc2tog in next 2 dc) 6 times. (12 sts)
Rnd 16: (dc2tog in next 2 dc) 6 times. (6 sts)
Rnd 17: (dc2tog in next 2 dc) 3 times. (3 sts)
Hook yarn and pull through these 3 sts to close.
Fasten off.

### Body
Make a magic ring.
Rnd 1: Work 6 dc into ring and pull it closed. (6 sts)
Rnd 2: 2 dc in each dc. (12 sts)
Rnd 3: (1 dc in next dc, 2 dc in next dc) 6 times. (18 sts)
Rnd 4: (1 dc in each of next 2 dc, 2 dc in next dc) 6 times. (24 sts)
Rnd 5: (1 dc in each of next 3 dc, 2 dc in next dc) 6 times. (30 sts)
Rnds 6-13: 1 dc in each dc. (8 rnds of 30 sts)
Rnd 14: (1 dc in each of next 3 dc, dc2tog in next 2 dc) 6 times. (24 sts)
Rnd 15: 1 dc in each dc. (24 sts)
Rnd 16: (1 dc in each of next 2 dc, dc2tog in next 2 dc) 6 times. (18 sts)
Fasten off.

### Ears (make 2)
Make a magic ring.
Rnd 1: 6 dc into ring and pull it closed. (6 sts)
Rnds 2-3: 1 dc in each dc (2 rnds of 6 sts)
Fasten off.

### Arms (make 2)
Make a magic ring.
Rnd 1: 5 dc into ring and pull it closed. (5 sts)
Rnd 2: 2 dc in each dc. (10 sts)
Rnd 3-12: 1 dc in each dc. (10 rnds of 10 sts)
Fasten off.

### Legs (make 2)
Make a magic ring.
Rnd 1: 8 dc into ring and pull it closed. (8 sts)
Rnd 2: 2 dc in each dc. (16 sts)
Rnd 3: 1 dc in each dc. (16 sts)
Rnd 4: 1 tr in each of next 6 dc, 1 dc in each of next 10 dc. (16 sts)
Rnd 5: (dc2tog in next 2 tr) 3 times, 1 dc in each of next 10 dc. (13 sts)
Rnds 6-13: 1 dc in each dc. (8 rnds of 13 sts)
Fasten off.

### Finishing
Stuff the body, arms and legs.
Sew the body to the head.
Sew the arms to the body between rnd 15 and rnd 16 and position them 6 sts apart in the front.
Sew the legs flat to the bottom of the body between rnd 2 and rnd 4, and position them close together in the front.

Designed by

## Amy Kember

Amy is a technical writer living in Ottawa, Canada. Her interest in crochet began when she discovered an amigurumi book in a used bookstore. After making a pig, she was instantly hooked. Since 2010, Amy has been designing and selling her own amigurumi patterns on Etsy. www.etsy.com/shop/AmysGurumis/

# Baby sloth

This darling critter loves hanging around. With tiny magnets in its paws, your baby sloth can hang just about anywhere!

## Difficulty

★★★☆☆

## What you need

- 3.25mm hook (US D/3)
- A pair of large (12mm) black plastic safety eyes
- Yarn needle
- Embroidery needle
- Fiberfill stuffing
- Dark brown and/or black embroidery thread
- Beige and dark brown felt
- Scissors
- 4 x 12mm neo magnets
- You will need to use DK weight yarn in your chosen colours. We have used Vanna's Choice by Lion Brand in:
  Colour 1: Barley (50g)
  Colour 2: Off white (oddment)
  Colour 3: Pink (oddment)

## Measurements

11.5cm tall.

Designed by
## Jasmin wang

Jasmin is an artist and crafter who enjoys painting, sewing, origami, and of course – crocheting! She loves bringing figures, ideas, and other concepts to life.
www.etsy.com/shop/Sylemn
www.facebook.com/SweetSofties

## Pattern

### Head and body

Using 3.25 mm hook and col 1, make a magic ring.
Rnd 1: 6 dc in magic ring, join with sl st. (6 sts)
Rnd 2: ch 1, 2 dc in each dc around, join with sl st. (12 sts)
Rnd 3: ch 1, (1 dc in next dc, 2 dc in next dc) 6 times, join with sl st. (18 sts)
Rnd 4: ch 1, (1 dc in each of next 2 dc, 2 dc in next dc) 6 times, join with sl st. (24 sts)
Rnd 5: ch 1, (1 dc in each of next 3 dc, 2 dc in next dc) 6 times, join with sl st. (30 sts)
Rnds 6-10: ch 1, dc around, join with sl st. (30 sts)
Rnd 11: ch 1, (1 dc in each of next 3 dc, dc2tog) 6 times, join with sl st. (24 sts)
Rnd 12: ch 1, (1 dc in each of next 6 dc, dc2tog) 3 times, join with sl st. (21 sts)
Rnd 13: ch 1, dc around, join with sl st. (21 sts)
Rnd 14: ch 1, (1 dc in each of next 6 dc, 2 dc in next dc) 3 times, join with sl st. (24 sts)
Rnd 15: ch 1, dc around, join with sl st. (24 sts)
Do not fasten off.

### Face

Using the pattern opposite (or your own!), cut out one face from beige felt and two eye patches from dark brown felt.
Make a hole in the eye patch by poking through with a yarn needle, or cutting small x slits with scissors. The holes will be for inserting plastic safety eyes.
Mark the eye location on the face, and make holes for fitting the plastic safety eyes.
Position the face over the sloth's head.
Make sure the tips of the safety eyes can be completely inserted.

Note: We have placed the face between rnd 6 and rnd 14. The eyes were positioned between rnd 10 and rnd 11.

Using blanket stitch, sew the face onto the sloth. Secure the safety eyes onto the sloth.

### Body (cont)

Continue crocheting the sloth's body.
Rnd 16: ch 1, (1 dc in each of next 7 dc, 2 dc in next dc) 3 times, join with sl st. (27 sts)
Rnd 17: ch 1, (1 dc in each of next 8 dc, 2 dc in next dc) 3 times, join with sl st. (30 sts)
Rnd 18: ch 1, (1 dc in each of next 9 dc, 2 dc in next dc) 3 times, join with sl st. (33 sts)
Rnds 19-20: ch 1, dc around, join . (33 sts)
Rnd 21: ch 1, (1 dc in each of next 9 dc, dc2tog) 3 times, join with sl st. (30 sts)
Rnd 22: ch 1, (1 dc in each of next 8 dc, dc2tog) 3 times, join with sl st. (27 sts)
Rnd 23: ch 1, (1 dc in each of next 7 dc, dc2tog) 3 times, join with sl st. (24 sts)
Begin stuffing the head and upper body firmly, but do not stretch the stitches.
Rnd 24: ch 1, (1 dc in each of next 2 dc, dc2tog) 6 times, join with sl st. (18 sts)
Rnd 25: ch 1, (1 dc in next dc, dc2tog) 6 times, join with sl st. (12 sts)
Finish stuffing the body.
Rnd 26: ch 1, dc2tog around, join with sl st. (6 sts)
Fasten off with a long tail, and stitch the bottom closed.

### Arms (make 2)

Using col 2, make a magic ring.
Rnd 1: 6 dc in magic ring, join with sl st. (6 sts)
Rnd 2: ch 1, 1 dc in each of next 3 dc, 2 dc in next dc, 1 dc in each of next 2 dc, join with sl st. (7 sts)
Rnds 3-4: ch 1, dc around, join with sl st. (7 sts)
Change to col 1.
Rnds 5-7: ch 1, dc around, join with sl st. (7 sts)
Do not fasten off yet. Push one magnet into the hand. Keep it in place by stitching through both layers of the hand using beige yarn.
Rnds 8-20: ch 1, dc around, join with sl st. (7 sts)
Fasten off, leaving a long tail for attaching to the body.

## Legs (make 2)

Follow instructions for rnds 1-18 of the arm. The legs are two rows shorter than the arms so not go to rnd 20.
Fasten off.

## Bow

Using col 3, ch 5.
Rnd 1: 1 dtr into 5th ch from hook (counts as ch 4 and 1 dtr), (3 dtr, ch 4 , sl st, ch 4, 4 dtr, ch 4, sl st) all into same ch.
Fasten off with a long tail for wrapping around the centre of the bow. Weave in the ends.

## Finishing

Place the arms and legs on the body. Make sure the magnets in the hands and feet stick together. Using a yarn needle, sew the pieces to the body.
Using brown yarn or embroidery thread, sew three lines over each paw.
Lastly, take the bow and sew it onto the sloth's head.

**Template (to size):**

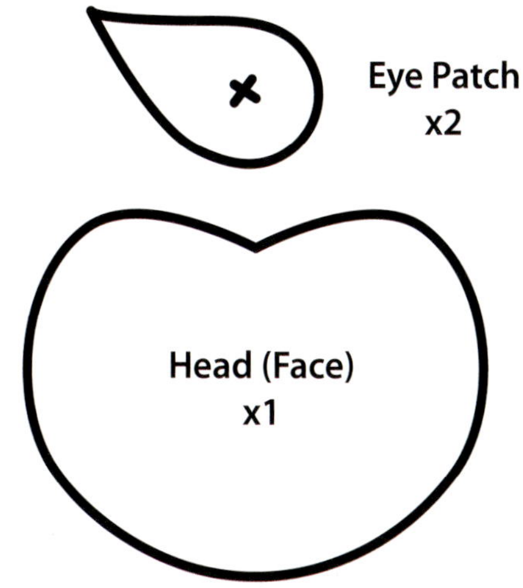

# Tiny princess

Create princesses, flower girls or bridesmaids that are quick to make, easily customisable and serve as lovely handmade gifts

## Difficulty

★★★☆☆

## What you need

- 13.25mm hook (US D/3)
- 1 pair 6mm plastic safety eyes
- Embroidery thread & needle
- Yarn needle
- Fiberfill stuffing
- Beads/pellets for weighted stuffing in the body
- Rose & ribbon
- You will need to use DK weight yarn in your chosen colours. We have used Caron's Simply Soft in:
  Colour 1 (skin): Light Country Peach (1 ball)
  Colour 2 (dress & hair tie): Fuchsia (1 ball)
  Colour 3 (hair): Gold (1 ball)

## Measurements

Approx 9.5cm tall

# Pattern

## Head

Using 3.25mm hook and col 1, make a magic ring.
Rnd 1: 6 dc in magic ring, join with ss. (6 sts)
Rnd 2: ch 1, 2 dc in each dc, join with ss. (12 sts)
Rnd 3: ch 1, (1 dc in next dc, 2 dc in next dc) 6 times, join with ss. (18 sts)
Rnd 4: ch 1, (1 dc in each of next 2 dc, 2 dc in next dc)
6 times, join with ss. (24 sts)
Rnds 5-9: ch 1, 1 dc around, join with ss. (5 rnds of 24 sts)
Rnd 10: ch 1, (1 dc in each of next 2 dc, dc2tog) 6 times, join with ss. (18 sts)
Rnd 11: ch 1, (1 dc in next dc, dc2tog) 6 times, join with ss. (12 sts)
Fasten off.
Stuff head firmly, but be careful not to stretch sts.

## Hair cap

Using col 3, make a magic ring.
Complete as for rnds 1-8 of head. Fasten off leaving a long tail for attaching to head later.

## Hair bun

Using col 3, make a magic ring.
Rnd 1: 6 dc in magic ring, join with ss. (6 sts)
Rnd 2: ch 1, 2 dc in each dc around, join with ss. (12 sts)
Rnd 3: ch 1, (1 dc in next 3 dc, 2 dc in next dc) 3 times, join with ss. (15 sts)
Rnds 4-5: ch 1, dc around, join with ss. (2 rnds of 15 sts)
Change to col 2 to create a contrasting hair tie/ribbon.
Rnd 6: ch 1, (1 dc in next 3 dc, dc2tog) 3 times, join with ss. (12 sts)
Fasten off, leaving a long tail for attaching to the hair cap later.

## Body

Using col 2, make a magic ring.
Rnd 1: 6 dc in magic ring, join with ss. (6 sts)
Rnd 2: ch 1, 2 dc in each dc around, join with ss. (12 sts)
Rnd 3: ch 1, (1 dc in next dc, 2 dc in next dc) 6 times, join with ss. (18 sts)
Rnd 4 (blo): ch 1, 1 dc in each dc, join with ss. (18 sts)
Rnd 5-6: ch 1, dc around, join with ss. (2 rnds of 18 sts)
Rnd 7: ch 1, (1 dc in each of next 7 dc, dc2tog) twice, join with ss. (16 sts)
Rnd 8: ch 1, 1 dc in each dc, join with ss. (16 sts)
Rnd 9: ch 1, (1 dc in each of next 6 dc, dc2tog) twice, join with ss. (14 sts)
Rnd 10: ch 1, 1 dc in each dc, join with ss. (14 sts)
Rnd 11: ch 1, (1 dc in each of next 5 dc, dc2tog) twice, join with ss. (12 sts)
Rnd 12: ch 1, 1 dc in each dc, join with ss. (12 sts)
Fasten off, leaving a long tail for attaching to the head later.

Note: When stuffing the body, add some beads/pellets to the bottom to provide some weight and stability, then stuff the rest of the body with fiberfill stuffing.

## Dress

Note: Dress is attached to the body.

Hold the body upside down (with the neck opening facing down).
Using col 2, attach yarn to the starting st on the bottom of the princess's body at rnd 9.
Rnd 1: ch 1, dc around, join with ss. (14 sts)
Rnd 2: 3 ch, (1 tr in each of next 6 tr, 2 tr in next tr) twice, join with ss. (16 sts)
Rnd 3: 3 ch, (1 tr in each of next 3 tr, 2 tr in next tr) 4 times, join with ss. (20 sts)
Rnd 4 (scalloped edging): ch 1, *1 dc in next tr, (1 htr, 1 tr) in next tr, (1 tr, 1 htr) in next tr, 1 dc in next tr; rep from * 5 times, join with ss. (5 scallops made)
Fasten off, and weave in ends.

## Arms (make 2)

Using col 1, ch 8.
1 dc into 2nd ch from hook,
1 dc into each ch to end. (7 dc)
Fasten off with tail for attaching.

## Finishing

Attach the pair of plastic safety eyes to the head (we put them between rnd 7 and rnd 8, 4 sts apart).
Using an embroidery needle and red/pink thread, sew a mouth onto the doll's face.
Using black thread, sew eyelashes to the corners of the eyes.
Stuff the hair bun lightly. Place the hair bun over the hair cap, and sew it on using a yarn needle. Then place the hair cap over the doll's head and sew it on. Attach your rose ribbon with a needle and thread.

Sew the arms onto the body, then sew the head firmly onto the body.
Fasten off.

Designed by
**Jasmin Wang**

Jasmin is an artist and crafter who enjoys painting, sewing, origami, and of course – crocheting! She loves bringing figures, ideas, and other concepts to life.
www.etsy.com/shop/Sylemn
www.facebook.com/SweetSofties

## Pattern notes

The Chain Loop Stitch is a wild-looking stitch that is deceptively easy to learn! In this pattern, the sheep's body is worked evenly with minimal increasing and decreasing, so you can just focus on learning the chain loop technique. The stitch is a great way to add texture to your crocheted work: use it to create fun fringe on garments, durable pom-poms, homemade dish scrubbies, hair for a doll, or other amigurumi animals (works great for hedgehogs)! Once you've become comfortable with the technique, try experimenting with varying chain lengths and spacing.

# Sleepy sheep

Crochet yourself this adorable and sleepy farm animal with chain loops

## Difficulty

★★★☆☆

## What you need

- 3.5mm hook (US E/4)
- Yarn needle
- Embroidery needle
- Black embroidery thread
- Pink embroidery thread
- Fiberfill stuffing
- You will need to use aran weight (worsted) yarn in two chosen colours. Here we have use Mondial Bio Soft in: Colour 1: Off-white (100g) Colour 2: Cream (100g)

## Measurements

10 cm long and 9 cm tall.

## Special stitches

Chain loop stitch: 1 dc in next st, ch 4.

Designed by

## Sarah Sloyer

When Sarah Sloyer first discovered amigurumi, she became determined to teach herself how to crochet so she could make them! After lots of practice, she is finally designing and writing her own patterns, which she loves sharing with others. She has more patterns available for free download and purchase at: ravelry.com/stores/critterbeans.

## Pattern

### Head and body

In col 1, make a magic ring.

Rnd 1 (RS): 6 dc into the magic ring. (6 sts)

Rnd 1: (1 dc in next st, 2 dc in next st) 3 times. (9 sts)

Rnd 2: (1 dc in next 2 sts, 2 dc in next st) 3 times. (12 sts)

Rnd 3: (1 dc in next 3 sts, 2 dc in next st) 3 times. (15 sts)

Rnd 4: (1 dc in next 4 sts, 2 dc in next st) 3 times. (18 sts)

Rnd 5: (1 dc in next 5 sts, 2 dc in next st) 3 times. (21 sts)

Rnd 6: (1 dc in next 6 sts, 2 dc in next st) 3 times. (24 sts)

Rnd 7: 1 dc in each st. (24 sts)

Rnd 8: 1 dc in next 5 sts, ch 8, re-insert hook into 5th dc (this is the st at the base of the ch 8) and ss to create ear, 1 dc in each of next 13 sts, ch 8, re-insert hook into the 13th st (this is the st at the base of the ch 8) and ss to create ear, 1 dc in next 5 sts, 1 dc in last st before marker, changing to col 2. (24 sts)

Embroider eyes, nose and mouth now.

Rnd 8: In col 2: (1 dc in next st, 2 dc in next st) 12 times. When you reach the ear loops from the previous round, make sure to push them forward and work behind them. (36 sts)

Rnd 9 (flo): (1 dc in next st, ch 4) 35 times, 1 dc in last st before marker but do not ch 4. (36 dc)

Rnd 10 (blo): In back loops leftover from previous rnd: 1 dc in each st. (36 sts)

Rnds 11-22: Rep Rnds 9-10 another 6 times. (36 sts)

Rnd 23 (flo): (1 dc in next st, ch 4) 35 times, 1 dc in last st before marker but do not ch 4. (36 sts)

Rnd 24: In back loops leftover from previous rnd: (1 dc in next 4 sts, dc2tog) 6 times. (30 sts)

Rnd 25 (flo): (1 dc in next st, ch 4) 29 times, 1 dc in last st before marker but do not ch 4. (30 sts)

Begin to stuff the sheep with fiberfill stuffing, continuing to stuff generously after completing the following rnds and until the end of the pattern.

Rnd 26: In back loops leftover from previous rnd: (1 dc in next 3 sts, dc2tog) 6 times. (24 sts)

Rnd 27 (flo): (1 dc in next st, ch 4) 23 times, 1 dc in last st before marker but do not ch 4. (24 sts)

Rnd 28: In back loops leftover from previous rnd: (dc in next 2 sts, dc2tog) 6 times. (18 sts)

Rnd 29 (flo): (1 dc in next st, ch 4) 17 times, 1 dc in last st before marker but do not ch 4. (18 sts)

Rnd 30: In back loops leftover from previous rnd: (1 dc in next st, dc2tog) 6 times. (12 sts)

Rnd 31 (flo): (1 dc in next st, ch 4) 11 times, 1 dc in last st before marker but do not ch 4. (12 sts)

Rnd 32: In back loops leftover from previous rnd: (dc2tog) 6 times. (6 sts)

Rnd 33 (flo): (1 dc in next st, ch 4) 5 times, 1 dc in last st before marker but do not ch 4. (6 sts)

Fasten off with a ss, leaving a tail. Thread your tail onto a yarn needle and weave it through each of the 6 left over back loops, pulling tight to close the hole. Weave in tail.

### Legs (make 4)

Using col 1, make a magic ring.

Rnd 1 (RS): 6 dc into the magic ring. (6 sts)

Rnds 2-5: 1 dc in each st. (6 sts)

Do not stuff. After completing Rnd 5, with your loop still on your hook, pinch the top of the leg flat and insert your hook through both sides of the leg and complete a dc. Repeat once more in the next stitch, through both sides, to close the top of the leg. Yo and pull through to fasten off, leaving a tail for sewing.

### Assembly

To attach each leg, thread the leftover yarn tail onto a yarn needle. Push apart the chain loop stitches to reveal the body of the sheep underneath. Insert your needle under the dc stitches, back out and through the stitches on the top of the leg. Repeat a few times until secure, then weave in and trim ends.

# Woodland turtle

With a fully detachable shell you can make this little turtle a different shell for every season

## Difficulty

★★★☆☆

## What you need

- 2.75mm hook (US C/2)
- Yarn needle
- Two 12mm black safety eyes
- Four 12mm safety eyes or doll joints for the limbs
- You will need to use worsted weight yarn in your chosen colours. We have used Rosario 4 Catitano in:
  Colour 1: Green (100g)
  Colour 2: Pale green (25g)
  Colour 3: Dark green (25g)
  Colour 4: Off white (50g)

## Measurements

Approximately 12.75cm tall, when seated, and 10cm wide

## Special stitches

Spike stitch: [SP] Instead of working a dc into the top of the stitch of the previous row or round, work into the stitch on the row or round below. You can do various lengths of spike stitches. Spike stitches are also known as long and dropped stitches.

Designed by

## Mevlinn Gusick

Mevlinn is a graduate with a BFA in Fine Arts Painting. Her interest in crochet began when a family member suggested crochet would be a great way to fill her spare time. Today she's crocheting amigurumi whenever she gets the chance and giving them to those she loves. www.mevvsan.com

## Pattern

### Head

Using 2.75mm hook and col 1, make a magic ring.
Rnd 1 (RS): 8 dc into the magic ring. (8 sts)
Rnd 2: 2 dc in each st. (16 sts)
Rnd 3: (2 dc in next st, 1 dc in next st) 8 times. (24 sts)
Rnd 4: (2 dc in next st, 1 dc in next 2 sts) 8 times. (32 sts)
Rnd 5: (2 dc in next st, 1 dc in next 3 sts) 8 times. (40 sts)
Rnd 6: 1 dc in each st. (40 sts)
Rnd 7: (2 dc in next st, 1 dc in next 4 sts) 8 times. (48 sts)
Rnds 8-16: 1 dc in each st. (48 sts)
Rnd 17: (dc2tog, 1 dc in next 4 sts) 8 times. (40 sts)
Rnd 18: (dc2tog, 1 dc in next 3 sts) 8 times. (32 sts)
Place 12mm black safety eyes between rnds 12-13 with 12 spaces between them.
Stuff with fiberfill and continue stuffing as you go.
Rnd 19: (dc2tog, 1 dc in next 2 sts) 8 times. (24 sts)
Rnd 20: (dc2tog, 1 dc in next st) 8 times. (16 sts)
Rnd 21: (dc2tog) 8 times. (8 sts)
Fasten off, leaving a tail for sewing. Using your yarn needle, weave the yarn tail through the front loop of each remaining st and pull it tight to close.
Embroider a small V shaped in between the two eyes for the mouth.

### Body

Using 2.75mm hook and col 1, make a magic ring.
Rnd 1 (RS): 6 dc into the magic ring. (6 sts)
Rnd 2: 2 dc in each st. (12 sts)
Rnd 3: (2 dc in next st, 1 dc in next st) 6 times. (18 sts)
Rnd 4: (2 dc in next st, 1 dc in next 2 sts) 6 times. (24 sts)
Rnd 5: (2 dc in next st, 1 dc in next 3 sts) 6 times. (30 sts)
Rnds 6-10: 1 dc in each st. (30 sts)
Rnd 11: (dc2tog, 1 dc in next 13 sts) twice. (28 sts)
Rnd 12: (dc2tog, 1 dc in next 12 sts) twice. (26 sts)
Rnd 13: (dc2tog, 1 dc in next 11 sts) twice. (24 sts)
Rnd 14: (dc2tog, 1 dc in next 10 sts) twice. (22 sts)
Rnd 15: (dc2tog, 1 dc in next 9 sts) twice. (20 sts)
Fasten off, leave a tail for sewing.

### Arms (make 2)

Using 2.75mm hook and col 1, make a magic ring.
Rnd 1 (RS): 4 dc into the magic ring. (4 sts)
Rnd 2: 2 dc in each st. (8 sts)
Rnds 3-11: 1 dc in each st. (8 sts)
Do not fasten off after rnd 11. Instead insert your 12mm black safety eye or doll joint inside the arm and have the post stick out between rnds 10 and 11. Lightly stuff the arm and continue crocheting Rnd 12.
Rnd 12: (dc2tog) 4 times. (4 sts)
Fasten off, leaving a tail for sewing. Weave in all yarn ends. When both arms are made they can be attached to the body around rnd 14 at equal distance from one another.

## Legs (make 2)

Using 2.75mm hook and col 1, make a magic ring.

Rnd 1 (RS): 5 dc into the magic ring. (5 sts)

Rnd 2: 2 dc in each st. (10 sts)

Rnds 3-13: 1 dc in each st. (10 sts)

Do not fasten off after rnd 13. Instead insert your 12mm black safety eye or doll joint inside the leg and have the post stick out between rnds 12 and 13. Lightly stuff the leg and continue crocheting rnd 14.

Rnd 14: (dc2tog) 5 times. (5 sts)

Fasten off, leaving a tail for sewing. Weave in all yarn ends. Attach both legs to the body around rnd 5. The joint should be inserted into the body directly below where the arm was placed.

You can now stuff the body and sew it onto the head.

## Tail

Using 2.75mm hook and col 1, ch 5.

Row 1 (RS): ss in second ch from hook, 1 dc in next ch, 1 htr in next ch, 1 dc in last ch. (4 sts)

Fasten off, leaving a tail for sewing. Sew the tail to the turtle's rump, around the magic ring.

## Shell

Note: The shell will be worked in the round, joining every round with a ss (not in a spiral). This means you will ss into the first st of every row then create a turning chain but you will not turn your work. The turning ch does not count as a st. This is done to improve the appearance of the colour change.

Using 2.75mm hook and col 2, make a magic ring.

Rnd 1 (RS): 6 dc into the magic ring, ss to first dc, ch 1. ( 6 sts)

Rnd 2: 2 dc in each st, ss to first dc, ch 1. (12 sts)

Change to col 3 at the last yarn over of the last dc in rnd 2. Do the same thing for every future colour change.

Row 3: (1 spike st through the centre of the magic ring, 2 dc in next st) 6 times, ss to first dc, ch 1. (18 sts) See Fig 1.

Rnd 4: (1 dc in next 2 sts, 2 dc in next st) 6 times, ss to first dc, ch 1. (24 sts)

Change to col 2.

Rnd 5: (1 spike st into rnd 3, the same row as the first spike st was made, that way the two spike sts look like they are touching, 1 dc in next 2 sts, 2 dc in next st) 6 times, ss to first dc, ch 1. (30 sts)

Rnd 6: (1 dc in next 4 sts, 2 dc in next st) 6 times, ss to first dc, ch 1. (36 sts)

Change to col 3.
Rnd 7: (1 spike st into rnd 5, 1 dc in next 5 sts) 6 times, ss to first dc, ch 1. (36 sts)
Rnd 8: 1 dc in each st, ss to first dc, ch 1. (36 sts) Change to col 2.
Rnd 9: (1 spike st into rnd 7, 1 dc in next 5 sts) 6 times, ss to first dc, ch 1. (36 sts)
Rnd 10: 1 dc in each st, ss to first dc, ch 1. (36 sts)

Note: Be sure to work with the right side of the shell facing you regardless of how you decided to crochet the rest of the project. The shell is crocheted like this so the colour changes are less noticeable.

You will now be working on closing the shell. There will be no more colour changes so you can start crocheting the shell in a spiral, without joining each rnd and no more turning chains. Change to col 3.
Rnd 11: BLO 1 dc in each st. (36 sts)
Rnd 12: 1 dc in next st (dc2tog, 1 dc in next 3 sts) 7 times. (29 sts)
Stuff lightly with fiberfill and continue stuffing as you go. Do not over stuff or the shell will not sit flat on the back.
Rnd 13: 1 dc in next st, (dc2tog, 1 dc in next 2 sts) 7 times. (22 sts)
Rnd 14: 1 dc in next st, (dc2tog, 1 dc in next st) 7 times. (15 sts)
Rnd 15: 1 dc in next st, (dc2tog) 7 times. (8 sts)
Fasten off, leaving a tail for sewing. Using your yarn needle, weave the yarn tail through the front loop of each remaining st and pull it tight to close.

## Shell edging

With the top of the shell facing you, attach col 2 in one of the unworked loops from rnd 10 of the shell and htr evenly around, ss to first st. (36 sts)
Fasten off and weave in ends

## Stomach shell

Using 2.75mm hook and col 4, ch 26.
Row 1 (RS): 1 dc in second ch from hook, 1 dc in each remaining ch, turn. (25 sts)
Row 2: ch 1 (not counted as a st here and throughout), dc2tog, 1 dc in next 21 sts, dc2tog, turn. (23 sts)
Rows 3-5: ch 1, 1 dc in each st, turn. (23 sts)
Fasten off, leaving a tail for sewing the two parts of the shell together when finished.

Note: Mark row 5 with stitch markers on the sixth st in on both the left and right side (Fig. 2) The 11 sts between these markers is where the top part of the stomach shell will continue, the 6 unworked sts on either side will make the arm holes.

## Top of stomach shell

With wrong side of the work facing you, attach col 4 in the st to the left of the marker.
Row 1: ch 1, 1 dc in same st, 1 dc in next 10 sts, turn. (11 sts)
Rows 2-3: ch 1, 1 dc in each st, turn. (11 sts)
Fasten off and weave in the yarn tail.
Mark the very first row of the stomach shell, which is the bottom, with two stitch markers 8 sts in from both sides. The 9 sts between these markers is where the bottom of the shell will be worked. The 8 unworked sts on each side will give room for the legs. (Fig. 2)

## Bottom of stomach shell

With wrong side facing you attach col 4 in the stitch to the left of the marker.
Row 1: ch 1, 1 dc in same st, 1 dc in next 8 sts, turn. (9 sts)
Row 2: ch 1, skip first st, 1 dc in next 6 sts, dc2tog. (7 sts)
Fasten off, leaving a tail for sewing the two parts of the shell together.
Use the two tails from creating the stomach shell to sew the two ends of the stomach shell to opposite sides of the main shell. This creates what looks like a "shirt" for your turtle. You can now slip the turtle's body though this shell and the shell will stay put due to the snug fit. You can secure with stitches if you prefer.

# Kimono doll

The Japanese Kimono Doll is an adorable kokeshi-style doll that makes a lovely friendship gift or décor in the home!

## Difficulty

★★★☆☆

## What you need

- 3.25mm hook (US D/3)
- 9mm plastic safety eyes
- Yarn needle
- Fiberfill stuffing
- Beads/pellets for weighted stuffing in body
- You will need to use worsted medium weight yarn, in your chosen colours. Here we have used Caron's Simply Soft in:
  Colour 1: Light Country Peach, 1 ball
  Colour 2: Black, 1 ball
  Colour 3: Strawberry, 1 ball
  Colour 4: Autumn Red, 1 ball
  Colour 5: Soft Pink, 1 ball
  Colour 6: Off white, oddments)

## Measurements

17cm tall.

Designed by
**Jasmin Wang**

Jasmin is an artist and crafter who enjoys painting, sewing, origami, and of course – crocheting! She loves bringing figures, ideas, and other concepts to life through the art of crochet.
www.etsy.com/shop/Sylemn,
www.Facebook.com/SweetSofties

## Pattern

### Head

Using 3.25mm hook and col 1, make a magic ring.

Rnd 1 (RS): 6 dc in magic ring. (6 sts)

Rnd 2: 2 dc in each st. (12 sts)

Rnd 3: (1 dc in next st, 2 dc in next st) 6 times. (18 sts)

Rnd 4: (1 dc in next 2 sts, 2 dc in next st) 6 times. (24 sts)

Rnd 5: (1 dc in next 3 sts, 2 dc in next st) 6 times. (30 sts)

Rnd 6: (1 dc in next 4 sts, 2 dc in next st) 6 times. (36 sts)

Rnd 7: (1 dc in next 11 sts, 2 dc in next st) 3 times. (39 sts)

Rnds 8-15: 1 dc in each st. (39 sts)

Rnd 16: (1 dc in next 11 sts, dc2tog) 3 times. (36 sts)

Rnd 17: (1 dc in next 4 sts, dc2tog) 6 times. (30 sts)

Rnd 18: (1 dc in next 3 sts, dc2tog) 6 times. (24 sts)

Rnd 19: (1 dc in next 2 sts, dc2tog) 6 times. (18 sts)

Stuff head firmly, but be careful not to stretch stitches.

Rnd 20: (1 dc in next st, dc2tog) 6 times. (12 sts)

Rnd 21: (dc2tog) 6 times. (6 sts)

Rnd 22: 1 dc in each st. (6 sts)

Fasten off.

### Hair cap

Using 3.25mm hook and col 2, make a magic ring.

Rnd 1 (RS): 6 dc in magic ring. (6 sts)

Rnd 2: 2 dc in each st. (12 sts)

Rnd 3: (1 dc in next st, 2 dc in next st) 6 times. (18 sts)

Rnd 4: (1 dc in next 2 sts, 2 dc in next st) 6 times. (24 sts)

Rnd 5: (1 dc in next 3 sts, 2 dc in next st) 6 times. (30 sts)

Rnd 6: (1 dc in next 4 sts, 2 dc in next st) 6 times. (36 sts)

Rnd 7: (1 dc in next 11 sts, 2 dc in next st) 3 times. (39 sts)

Rnds 8-11: 1 dc in each st. (39 sts)

### Hair bun

Using 3.25mm hook and col 2, make a magic ring.

Rnd 1 (RS): 6 dc in magic ring, ss to first dc to join. (6 sts)

Rnd 2: ch 1 (not counted as a st throughout), 2 dc in each st, ss to first dc. (12 sts)

Rnd 3: ch 1, (1 dc in next st, 2 dc in next st) 6 times, ss to first dc. (18 sts)

Rnd 4: ch 1, (1 dc in next 2 sts, 2 dc in next st) 6 times, ss to first dc. (24 sts)

Rnd 5: ch 1, (1 dc in next 3 sts, 2 dc in next st) 6 times, ss to first dc. (30 sts)

Rnds 6-8: ch 1, 1 dc in each st, ss to first dc. (30 sts)

Rnd 9: ch 1, (1 dc in next 3 sts, dc2tog) 6 times, ss to first dc. (24 sts)

Change to col 3.

Rnd 10: ch 1, (1 dc in next 2 sts, dc2tog) 6 times, ss to first dc. (18 sts)

Fasten off, leaving a long tail for attaching to hair cap.

### Sleeves (make 2)

Using 3.25mm hook and col 3, ch 11.

Rnd 1 (RS): ch 1 (not counted as a st throughout), 1 dc in 2nd ch from hook, 1 dc in next 8 ch, 3 dc in last ch, rotate and work along opposite side of starting chain (into the spare loops), 1 dc in next 8 ch, 2 dc in last ch, ss to first dc to join. (22 sts)

Rnd 2: ch 1, 2 dc in next st, 1 dc in next 8 sts, 2 dc in next 3 sts, 1 dc in next 8 sts, 2 dc in next 2 sts, ss to first dc. (28 sts)

Rnd 3: ch 1, 1 dc in next st, 2 dc in next st, 1 dc in next 9 sts, (2 dc in next st, 1 dc in next st) twice, 2 dc in next st, 1 dc in next 9 sts, 2 dc in next st, 1 dc in next st, 2 dc in next st, ss to first dc. (34 sts)

Rnd 4: ch 1, 2 dc in next 2 sts, 1 dc in next 11 sts, 2 dc in next 2 sts, 1 dc in next 2 sts, 2 dc in next 2 sts, 1 dc in next 11 sts, 2 dc in next 2 sts, 1 dc in next 2 sts, ss to first dc. (42 sts)

Rnd 5: ch 1, (2 dc in next st, 1 dc in next st) twice, 1 dc in next 12 sts, (2 dc in next st, 1 dc in next st) twice, 1 dc in next st, (2 dc in next st, 1 dc in next st) twice, 1 dc in next 12 sts, (2 dc in next st, 1 dc in next st) twice, 1 dc in next st, ss to first dc. (50 sts)
Rnd 6: ch 1, (1 dc in next 2 sts, 2 dc in next st) twice, 1 dc in next 11 sts, (2 dc in next st, 1 dc in next 2 sts) twice, 1 dc in next 4 sts, (2 dc in next st, 1 dc in next 2 sts) twice, 1 dc in next 9 sts, (2 dc in next st, 1 dc in next 2 sts) twice,1 dc in next 2 sts, ss to first dc. (58 sts)
Fasten off .

## Body wrap

Using 3.25mm hook and col 3, ch 30.
Rnd 1: ch 1, dc in 2nd ch from hook, 1 dc in next 27 ch, 3 dc in next ch, rotate and work along opposite side of starting ch (into the spare loops), 1 dc in next 27 ch, 2 dc in last ch, ss to first dc to join. (60 sts)
Rnd 2: ch 1, 2 dc in next st, 1 dc in next 27 sts, 2 dc in next 3 sts, 1 dc in next 27 sts, 2 dc in next 2 sts, ss to first dc. (66 sts)
Rnd 3: ch 1, 1 dc in next st, 2 dc in next st, 1 dc in next 28 sts, (2 dc in next st, 1 dc in next st) 3 times, 1 dc in next 27 sts, 2 dc in next st, 1 dc in next st, 2 dc in next st, ss to first dc to join. (72 sts)
Rnd 4: ch 1, 2 dc in next 2 sts, (1 dc in next 4 sts, dc2tog) twice, 1 dc in next 6 sts, (dc2tog, 1 dc in next 4 sts) twice, (2 dc in next 2 sts, 1 dc in next 2 sts) twice, 1 dc in next 3 sts, 2 dc in next st, 1 dc in next 4 sts, 2 dc in next st, 1 dc in next 8 sts, 2 dc in next st, 1 dc in next 4 sts, 2 dc in next st, 1 dc in next 5 sts, 2 dc in next 2 sts, 1 dc in next 2 sts, ss to first dc. (80 sts)
Rnd 5: ch 1, (2 dc in next st, 1 dc in next st) twice, 1 dc in next 2 sts, (dc2tog, 1 dc in next 3 sts) 5 times, (2 dc in next st, 1 dc in next st) twice, 1 dc in next st, (2 dc in next st, 1 dc in next st) twice, 1 dc in next 7 sts, 2 dc in next st, 1 dc next 9 sts, (2 dc in next st, 1 dc in next 8 sts) twice, 2 dc in next st, 1 dc in next st, 2 dc in next st, 1 dc in next 2 sts, ss to first dc. (86 sts)
Rnd 6: ch 1, 1 dc in next 2 sts, 2 dc in next st, 1 dc in next 27 sts, 2 dc in next st, 1 dc in next 6 sts, 2 dc in next st, 1 dc in next 2 sts, 2 dc in next st, 1 dc in next 37 sts, 2 dc in next st, 1 dc in next 2 sts, 2 dc in next st, 1 dc in next 4 sts, ss to first dc. (92 sts)
Change to col 4.
Rnd 7: ch1, 1 dc in next 40 sts, 2 dc in next 2 sts, 1 dc in next 42 sts, 2 dc in next 2 sts, 1 dc in next 6 sts, ss to first dc. (96 sts)
Fasten off.

## Arms (make 2)

Using 3.25mm hook and col 1, make a magic ring.
Rnd 1 (RS): 6 dc in magic ring. (6 sts)
Rnd 2: (1 dc in next st, 2 dc in next st) 3 times. (9 sts)
Rnds 3-7: 1 dc in each st. (9 sts)
Dc2tog twice and fasten off.

## Body

Using 3.25mm hook and col 5, make a magic ring.
Rnd 1: 6 dc in magic ring, ss to first dc. (6 sts)
Rnd 2:
ch 1, 2 dc in each st, ss to first dc. (12 sts)
Rnd 3: ch 1, (1 dc in next st, 2 dc in next st) 6 times, ss to first dc. (18 sts)
Rnd 4: ch 1, (1 dc in next 2 sts, 2 dc in next st) 6 times, ss to first dc. (24 sts)
Rnd 5: ch 1, (1 dc in next 3 sts, 2 dc in next st) 6 times, ss to first dc. (30 sts)
Rnd 6: ch 1, (1 dc in next 4 sts, 2 dc in next st) 6 times, ss to first dc. (36 sts)
Rnd 7 (blo): ch 1, 1 dc in BLO of each st, ss to first dc. (36 sts)
Rnds 8-12: ch 1, 1 dc in each st, ss to first dc. (36 sts)
Rnd 13: ch 1, (1 dc in next 4 sts, dc2tog) 6 times, ss to first dc. (30 sts)
Rnd 14: ch 1, 1 dc in each st, ss to first dc. (30 sts)
Rnd 15: ch 1, (1 dc in next 3 sts, dc2tog) 6 times, ss to first dc. (24 sts)
Change to col 6.
Rnd 16-17: ch 1, 1 dc in each st, ss to first dc. (24 sts)
Rnd 18: ch 1, (1 dc in next 2 sts, dc2tog) 6 times, ss to first dc. (18 sts)
Rnd 19-20: ch 1, 1 dc in each st, ss to first dc. (18 sts)

**Top Tip**
Change the colour variation, add embroidering or embellishments such as buttons, bows, and hair accessories, or try different hairstyles to make this little doll your very own!

Rnd 21: ch 1, (1 dc in next st, dc2tog) 6 times, ss to first dc. (12 sts)
Rnd 22: ch 1, 1 dc in each st, ss to first dc. (12 sts)
Fasten off, leaving a long tail for attaching to head. When stuffing the body, add some beads/pellets to the bottom to give this top-heavy amigurumi some weight and stability. Then, stuff the rest of the body with fiberfill stuffing.

## Bow

Using 3.25mm hook and col 4, ch 20, ss to first ch to join into a ring.
Rnd 1: ch 1, 1 dc in same st, 1 dc in each ch, ss to first dc. (20 sts)
Rnd 2-5: ch 1, 1 dc in same st, 1 dc in each st, ss to first dc. (20 sts)
Fasten off with a very long tail. Tightly wrap it multiple times around the middle of the crocheted rectangle, in order to form the bow shape.

## Belt

Using 3.25mm hook and col 4, make a chain that fits snugly around the doll's body and body wrap.
Rnd 1: 1 dc in 2nd ch from hook, 1 dc in each ch.
Fasten off, leaving a long tail for attaching to other end of belt.

## Flower hair accessory

Using 3.25mm hook and flower col 6, make a magic ring.
Rnd 1: 5 dc in magic ring, ss to first dc to join. (5 sts)
Rnd 2: *ch 2, (2 dc, ch 2, ss) all into same st, ss in next st; rep from * 4 more times.
Fasten off, leaving a tail.

## Finishing

Attach plastic safety eyes to the head.
Sew the eyelashes and mouth using either embroidery thread or yarn.

Note: If you want, add blush to doll's cheeks. We recommend using actual blush powder applied with a paintbrush or finger. Alternatively, you could use a red pencil.

Stuff the hair bun lightly. Carefully position it onto the hair cap and sew it on. Sew the hair cap onto the head.
Sew the flower hair accessory securely onto the doll's hair, next to her hair bun.

Note: Sew a button or bead into the center of the flower for an extra touch.

Using black yarn, sew the fringe onto the head.
If desired, embroider designs or attach beads to the kimono sleeves and body wrap.
Take the oval sleeves and fold them in half. Place arms inside of the sleeves and sew them securely. Attach col 4 at opposite end of sleeve. Dc around the back with sleeves held together. Stop more than halfway around the semi-circle sleeve, do not fasten off.
Continue by dc around separate flaps near the arms, and ss to join.
Sew the wrap to the body, followed by the belt. Then attach the bow to the back of the body and belt. Sew the sleeves/arms to the body. Finally sew the head to the body.

# Ginger the giraffe

Ginger the giraffe is an adorable, safari plush that makes for a lovely, handmade gift for babies, children, and giraffe fans!

## Difficulty

★★★☆☆

## What you need

- 3.25mm hook (US D/3)
- A pair of large (12mm) black plastic safety eyes
- Yarn needle
- Fiberfill stuffing
- Hair grips
- Scissors
- You will need to use worsted weight yarn, in your chosen colours. Here we have used Caron's Super Soft in:
  Colour 1: Yellow (100g)
  Colour 2: Light brown (50g)
  Colour 3: Brown (50g)

## Measurements

27cm tall.

Designed by
**Jasmin Wang**

Jasmin is an artist and crafter who enjoys painting, sewing, origami, and of course – crocheting! She loves bringing figures, ideas, and other concepts to life through the art of crochet.
www.etsy.com/shop/Sylemn,
www.Facebook.com/SweetSofties

## Pattern

### Head

Using 3.25mm hook and col 1, make a magic ring.

Rnd 1(RS): 6 dc into the magic ring, ss to first dc. (6 sts)
Rnd 2: ch 1, 2 dc in each st, ss first dc. (12 sts)
Rnd 3: ch 1, (1 dc in next st, 2 dc in next st) 6 times, ss to first dc. (18 sts)
Rnd 4: ch 1, (1 dc in next 2 sts, 2 dc in next st) 6 times, ss to first dc. (24 sts)
Rnd 5: ch 1, (1 dc in next 3 sts, 2 dc in next st) 6 times, ss to first dc. (30 sts)
Rnd 6: ch 1, (1 dc in next 4 sts, 2 dc in next st) 6 times, ss to first dc. (36 sts)
Rnd 7: ch 1, (1 dc in next 5 sts, 2 dc in next st) 6 times, ss to first dc. (42 sts)
Rnd 8: ch 1, (1 dc in next 6 sts, 2 dc in next st) 6 times, ss to first dc. (48 sts)
Rnd 9: ch 1, (1 dc in next 7 sts, 2 dc in next st) 6 times, ss to first dc. (54 sts)
Rnd 10: ch1, (1 dc in next 8 sts, 2 dc in next st) 6 times, ss to first dc. (60 sts)
Rnds 11-19: ch 1, 1 dc in each st, ss to first dc. (60 sts)
Rnd 20: ch 1, (1 dc in next 8 sts, dc2tog) 6 times, ss to first dc. (54 sts)
Rnd 21: ch 1, (1 dc in next 7 sts, dc2tog) 6 times, ss to first dc. (48 sts)
Rnd 22: ch 1, (1 dc in next 6 sts, dc2tog) 6 times, ss to first dc. (42 sts)
Rnd 23: ch 1, (1 dc in next 5 sts, dc2tog) 6 times, ss to first dc. (36 sts)
Rnd 24: ch 1,(1 dc in next 4 sts, dc2tog) 6 times, ss to first dc. (30 sts)
Rnd 25: ch 1, (1 dc in next 3 sts, dc2tog) 6 times, ss to first dc. (24 sts)

Fasten off with a long tail for attaching to the body. Stuff the head firmly, but be careful not to stretch the stitches.

### Snout

Using 3.25mm hook and col 2, ch 8.

Rnd 1 (RS): 1 dc in 2nd ch from hook and in each of next 6 ch (in outer loops only), continue around the other side of the chain, 1 dc in each outer loop, ss to first dc to join. (14 sts).
Rnd 2: ch 1, (1 dc in next st, 2 dc in next st) 7 times, ss to first dc. (21 sts)
Rnd 3: ch 1, (1 dc in next 2 sts, 2 dc in next st) 7 times, ss to first dc. (28 sts)
Rnd 4: ch 1, 1 dc in each st, ss to first dc. (28 sts)

Fasten off with a long tail for attaching to the head later.

### Ears (make 2)

Using 3.25mm hook and col 1, make a magic ring.

Rnd 1 (RS): 6 dc into the magic ring, ss to first dc. (6 sts)
Rnd 2: ch 1, 2 dc in each st, ss to first dc. (12 sts)
Rnd 3: ch 1, (1 dc in next st, 2 dc in next st) 6 times, ss to first dc. (18 sts)
Rnds 4-7: ch 1, 1 dc in each st, ss to first dc. (18 sts)

Fasten off with a long tail for attaching to the body later. Ears do not need to be stuffed, but will be folded in half when sewn onto the head.
Then, stuff the rest of the body.

### Ossicones (make 2)

Using col 3, make a magic ring.

Rnd 1 (RS): 6 dc into the magic ring, ss to first dc. (6 sts)
Rnd 2: ch 1, 2 dc in each st, ss to first dc. (12 sts)
Rnd 3: ch 1, 1 dc in each st, ss to first dc. (12 sts)
Rnd 4: ch 1, (dc2tog) 6 times, ss to first dc. (6 sts)
Change to col 1.
Rnds 5-7: ch 1, 1 dc in each st, ss to first dc. (6 sts)

Fasten off with a long tail for attaching to the head later. Stuff lightly.

## Arms (make 2)

Using 3.25mm hook and col 3, make a magic ring.
Rnd 1: 6 dc into the magic ring, ss to first dc. (6 sts)
Rnd 2: ch 1, 2 dc in each st, ss to first dc. (12 sts)
Rnd 3: ch 1, (1 dc in next st, 2 dc in next st) 6 times, ss to first dc. (18 sts)
Rnds 4-6: ch 1, 1 dc in each st, ss to first dc. (18 sts)
Change to col 1.
Rnds 7-9: ch 1, 1 dc in each st, ss to first dc. (18 sts)
Rnd 10: ch 1, (1 dc in next 7 sts, dc2tog) twice, ss to first dc. (16 sts)
Rnds 11-13: ch 1, 1 dc in each st, ss to first dc. (16 sts)
Rnd 14: ch 1, (1 dc in next 6 sts, dc2tog) twice, ss to first dc. (14 sts)
Rnds 15-17: ch 1, 1 dc in each st, ss to first dc. (14 sts)
Rnd 18: ch 1, (1 dc in next 5 sts, dc2tog) twice, ss to first dc. (12 sts)
Rnds 19-20: ch 1, 1 dc in each st, ss to first dc. (12 sts)
Rnd 21: Without fastening off, pinch the end of the arm shut. Stitch across that row to close it, by doing the following: ch 1, 1 dc in next 6 sts. (6 sts)
Fasten off with a long tail for attaching to the body.

## Legs (make 2)

Note: The legs and body are worked in one piece, starting with the legs. Do not fasten off until instructed to do so.

Using 3.25mm hook and col 1, make magic ring.
Rnd 1 (RS): 6 dc into the magic ring, ss to first dc. (6 sts)
Rnd 2: ch 1, 2 dc in each st, ss to first dc.. (12 sts)
Rnd 3: ch 1, (1 dc in next st, 2 dc in next st) 6

times, ss to first dc. (18 sts)
Rnd 4: ch 1, (1 dc in next 2 sts, 2 dc in next st) 6 times, ss to first dc. (24 sts)
Rnd 5: ch 1, (1 dc in next 7 sts, 2 dc in next st) 3 times, ss to first dc. (27 sts)
Rnds 6-10: ch 1,1 dc in each st, ss to first dc. (27 sts)
Make two legs. Fasten off for the first leg, but do not fasten off for second leg. Instead, continue with instructions for the pelvic area.

## Pelvic area

With yarn still attached to the second leg, ch 3.
Insert hook into first st of first leg. Yarn over to pull through a sl st. Now, you've joined the legs together. Continue working on the body.

## Body portion

Note: In rnd 1, you will dc around both legs and the middle chain.

Rnd 1 (RS): ch 1, 1 dc in next st, and around the first leg for a total of 27 sts. Continue to dc in the outer loops of the middle chain for total of 3 sts. Continue to dc around the second leg for a total of 27 sts. Continue to dc in the outer loops of the middle chain for a total of 3 sts, ss to first dc. (60 sts)
Rnd 2: ch 1, (1 dc in next 9 sts, 2 dc in next st) 6 times, ss to first dc. (66 sts)
Rnds 3-7: ch 1, 1 dc in each st, ss to first dc. (66 sts)
Rnd 8: ch 1, (1 dc in next 20 sts, dc2tog) 3 times, ss to first dc. (63 sts)
Rnd 9: ch 1, 1 dc in each st, ss to first dc. (63 sts)
Rnd 10: ch 1, (1 dc in next 19 sts, dc2tog) 3 times, ss to first dc. (60 sts)
Rnd 11: ch 1, 1 dc in each st, ss to first dc. (60 sts)
Rnd 12: ch 1, (1 dc in next 8 sts, dc2tog) 6 times, ss to first dc. (54 sts)
Rnd 13: ch 1, 1 dc in each st, ss to first dc. (54 sts)
Rnd 14: ch 1, (1 dc in next 7 sts, dc2tog) 6 times, ss to first dc. (48 sts)
Rnd 15: ch 1, 1 dc in each st, ss to first dc. (48 sts)
Rnd 16: ch 1, (1 dc in next 6 sts, dc2tog) 6 times, ss to first dc. (42 sts)
Rnd 17: ch 1, 1 dc in each st, ss to first dc. (42 sts)
Rnd 18: ch 1, (1 dc in next 5 sts, dc2tog) 6 times, ss to first dc. (36 sts)
Rnd 19: ch 1, 1 dc in each st, ss to first dc. (36 sts)
Rnd 20: ch 1, (1 dc in next 4 sts, dc2tog) 6 times, ss to first dc. (30 sts)
Rnd 21: ch 1, 1 dc in each st, ss to first dc. (30 sts)
Rnd 22: ch 1, (1 dc in next 13 sts, dc2tog) twice, ss to first dc. (28 sts)
Rnd 23: ch 1, 1 dc in each st, ss to first dc. (28 sts)
Rnd 24: ch 1, (1 dc in next 12 sts, dc2tog) twice, ss to first dc. (26 sts)
Rnd 25: ch 1, 1 dc in each st, ss to first dc. (26 sts)
Rnd 26: ch 1, (1 dc in next 11 sts, dc2tog) twice, ss to first dc. (24 sts)
Rnds 27-31: ch 1, 1 dc in each st, ss to first dc. (24 sts)
Fasten off and stuff the body firmly, but be careful not to stretch the stitches. Set aside for finishing directions.

## Spots

Using 3.25mm hook and col 3 make magic ring.
Rnd 1: 4 dc into the magic ring, ss to first dc. (4 sts)
Rnd 2: 2dc in each st around (8sts)
Rnd 3: (1dc in next st, 2dc in next st) 4 times (12 sts)
Fasten off.

## Finishing

Position the ossicones, ears, and snout on the head. Gently stuff the snout. Use hair grips to help keep the pieces secure and help give a good idea of placement.
Next, sew the pieces onto the head using a yarn needle and the long yarn tails from each of the pieces.
Attach the 12mm safety eyes onto the head.
Position the arms on the body, and arrange the spots where you'd like them. Again, use hair grips to keep them secure.
Sew the pieces onto the body.
Last, sew the head onto the body.

Designed by

## Mevlinn Gusick

Mevlinn is a college graduate with a BFA in Fine Arts Painting. Her interest in knitting and crochet began when her aunt suggested she try knitting. It piqued her curiosity and here she is today, crocheting amigurumi whenever she gets the chance and giving them to those she loves.
www.mevvsan.com

# Horace the monster

It's hard to believe but Horace has terrible eye sight, he can't see more than a foot away from his face. Sadly, he can't seem to find a pair of glasses that will fit

## Difficulty

★★★★☆

## What you need

- 2.75mm hook (US C/2)
- Safety eyes: five x 18mm, six x 9mm, four x 12mm
- Fiberfill stuffing
- White felt for the tooth
- Glue to attach the tooth
- You will need an Aran weight yarn. We have used Rosario 4: Catitano in:
  Colour 1: White (50g)
  Colour 2: Blue (50g)
  Colour 3: Dark blue (50g)
  Colour 4: Grey (50g)
  Colour 5: Yellow (50g)

## Measurements

28 cm tall, while standing, and 12.75 cm wide.

## Special stitches

Surface crochet: crocheting directly into the body of the amigurumi.
3 dtr popcorn stitch: work a dtr to the last yarn over (2 loop left on hook), stop and create two more incomplete dtr sts. You should have 4 loops on your hook. yo and pull through all loops.
2 tr popcorn stitch: work a tr to the last yarn over (2 loops left on hook), stop and create one more incomplete trst. You should have 3 loops on your hook. Yo and pull through all loops.

## Pattern

Note: Be aware that when you work with the wrong side out the front and back loops of a stitch will be reversed. When you see instructions written as "flo (blo)" in this pattern, you will work what is before the brackets if you are crocheting with the right side out, and you will work what is in the brackets if you are working with the wrong side facing out.

## Small eye (make 6)

Using 2.75mm hook and col 1, make a magic ring.
Rnd 1 (RS): 5 dc into the magic ring. (5 sts)
Place your 9mm safety eye in the middle of the magic ring and pull the ring tight around the post. After rnd 2, fix the back of the safety eye in place.
Rnd 2: 2 dc in each st. (10 sts)
Change to col 2.
Rnds 3-5: 1 dc in each st. (10 sts)
Stuff with fiberfill and continue stuffing as you go.
Rnd 6: (dc2tog) 5 times. (5 sts)
Fasten off, leaving a long tail for sewing.
Using your yarn needle, weave the yarn tail through the front loop of each remaining stitch and pull it tight to close. Do not cut yarn.
For the rim, have the white of the small eye facing you, think of the eye as a clock, and attach col 2 at the 12 o'clock position between rnds 2-3.

Note: If you attach the yarn at 6 o'clock the eye rim will be reversed and incorrect.

Rnd 1 (RS): ch 1 (not counted as a st here and throughout), 1 dc in next 10 sts, ss into first dc. (10 sts)
Rnd 2: ch 1, (2 dc in next st, 1 dc in next 4 sts) twice, ss into first dc. (12 sts) (See Fig. 2)
Fasten off and darn in all ends.

## Medium eye (make 4)

Using 2.75mm hook and col 1, make a magic ring.
Rnd 1 (RS): 5 dc into the magic ring. (5 sts)
Place your 12mm safety eye in the middle of the magic ring and pull the ring tight around the post. After rnd 2, fix the back of the safety eye in place.
Rnd 2: 2 dc in each st. (10 sts)
Rnd 3: (2 dc in next st, 1 dc in next st) 5 times. (15 sts)
Change to col 2.
Rnds 4-6: 1 dc in each st. (15 sts)
Rnd 7: (dc2tog, 1 dc in next st) 5 times. (10 sts)
Stuff with fiberfill and continue stuffing as you go.
Rnd 8: (dc2tog) 5 times. (5 sts)
Fasten off, leaving a long tail for sewing.
Using your yarn needle, weave the yarn tail through the front loop of each remaining stitch and pull it tight to close. Leave the remaining yarn tail so you can use it to sew the eye to the body later.
Complete the rim of the eye as you did for the small eye.
Rnd 1 (RS): ch 1 (not counted as a st here and throughout), 1 dc in next 15 sts, ss into first dc. (15 sts)
Rnd 2: ch 1, (2 dc in next st, 1 dc in next 4 sts) 3 times, ss into first st. (18 sts) (See Fig. 2)
Fasten off and weave in all yarn ends.

## Large eye (make 5)

Using 2.75mm hook and col 1, make a magic ring.
Rnd 1 (RS): 5 dc into the magic ring. (5 sts)
Place your 18mm safety eye in the middle of the magic ring and pull the ring tight around the post. After rnd 2, fix the back of the safety eye in place.
Rnd 2: 2 dc in each st. (10 sts)
Rnd 3: (2 dc in next st, 1 dc in next st) 5 times. (15 sts)

Rnd 4: (2 dc in next st, 1 dc in next 2 sts) 5 times. (20 sts)
Change to col 2.
Rnds 5-7: 1 dc in each st. (20 sts)
Rnd 8: (dc2tog, 1 dc in next 2 sts) 5 times. (15 sts)
Stuff with fiberfill and continue stuffing as you go.
Rnd 9: (dc2tog, 1 dc in next st) 5 times. (10 sts)
Rnd 10: (dc2tog) 5 times. (5 sts)
Fasten off, leaving a long tail for sewing. Using your yarn needle, weave the yarn tail through the front loop of each remaining stitch and pull it tight to close. Leave the remaining yarn tail so you can use it to sew the eye to the body later.
Complete the rim of the eye as you did for the small eye.
Rnd 1 (RS): ch 1 (not counted as a st here and throughout), 1 dc in next 20 sts, ss into first dc. (20 sts)
Rnd 2: ch 1, (2 dc in next st, 1 dc in next 4 sts) 4 times, ss into first dc. (24 sts) (See Fig. 2)
Fasten off and darn in all ends.

## Body

Using 2.75mm hook and col 2, make a magic ring.
Rnd 1 (RS): 8 dc into the magic ring. (8 sts)
Rnd 2: 2 dc in each st. (16 sts)
Rnd 3: (2 dc in next st, 1 dc in next st) 8 times. (24 sts)
Rnd 4: (2 dc in next st, 1 dc in next 2 sts) 8 times. (32 sts)
Rnd 5: (2 dc in next st, 1 dc in next 3 sts) 8 times. (40 sts)
Rnd 6: (2 dc in next st, 1 dc in next 4 sts) 8 times. (48 sts)
Rnd 7: 1 dc in each st. (48 sts)
Rnd 8: (2 dc in next st, 1 dc in next 5 sts) 8 times. (56 sts)
Rnds 9-12: 1 dc in each st. (56 sts)
Rnd 13: (dc2tog, 1 dc in next 12 sts) 4 times. (52 sts)
Rnd 14: 1 dc in each st. (52 sts)
Rnd 15: (dc2tog, 1 dc in next 11 sts) 4 times. (48 sts)
Rnd 16: 1 dc in each st. (48 sts)
Rnd 17: (dc2tog, 1 dc in next 10 sts) 4 times. (44 sts)
Rnd 18: 1 dc in each st. (44 sts)
Rnd 19: (dc2tog, 1 dc in next 9 sts) 4 times. (40 sts)
Rnd 20: 1 dc in each st. (40 sts)
Rnd 21: (dc2tog, 1 dc in next 8 sts) 4 times. (36 sts)

Stuff with fiberfill and continue stuffing as you go.
Rnd 22 BLO (FLO): 1dc in next 9 sts, 1 dc in both loops of remaining 27 sts. (36 sts)
Rnd 23: 1 dc in each st. (36 sts)
Rnd 24: (dc2tog, 1 dc in next 7 sts) 4 times. (32 sts)
Rnds 25-26: 1 dc in each st. (32 sts)
Rnd 27: (dc2tog, 1 dc in next 6 sts) 4 times. (28 sts)
Rnds 28-29: 1 dc in each st. (28 sts)
Rnd 30: (dc2tog, 1 dc in next 5 sts) 4 times. (24 sts)
Rnds 31-32: 1 dc in each st. (24 sts)
Rnd 33: (dc2tog, 1 dc in next 4 sts) 4 times. (20 sts)
Rnds 34-35: 1 dc in each st. (20 sts)
Rnd 36: (dc2tog, 1 dc in next 2 sts) 5 times. (15 sts)
Rnd 37: (dc2tog, 1 dc in next st) 5 times. (10 sts)
Rnd 38: (dc2tog) 5 times. (5 sts)
Fasten off, leaving a tail for sewing. Using your yarn needle, weave the yarn tail through the front loop of each remaining stitch and pull it tight to close.

## Body lines

With the back of the body facing you, attach col 3 between rnds 17-16. (Fig 3) Begin to surface crochet by slip stitching evenly around the body until you reach the point you started from. ss into first st and fasten off. Weave in all ends.
Repeat this for the remaining 4 lines starting with col 4 for between rnds 16-15, col 5 for rnds 15-14, col 4 for rnds 14-13 and col 3 for rnds 13-12.

## Mouth

Using 2.75mm hook and col 2, ss into the first unworked loop from rnd 22 of the body on the far right side. 1 dc into the same st, 1 htr in each st until the second to last st, 1 dc in next st, ss in the last st. Fasten off, weave in all yarn ends.

## Tooth

Cut a small triangle out of white felt and glue it with some craft or fabric glue so the lip of the mouth overlaps it.

## Foot and leg (make 2)

Using 2.75m hook and col 2, make a magic ring.
Rnd 1 (RS): 6 dc into the magic ring. (6 sts)
Rnd 2: 2 dc in each st. (12 sts)
Rnd 3: (2 dc in next st, 1 dc in next st) 6 times. (18 sts)
Rnd 4: (3 dtr popcorn st in next st, 1 dc in next st) 4 times (See Fig. 4), dc in next 10 sts. (18 sts)
Rnd 5: 1 dc in each st. (18 sts)
Rnd 6: (dc2tog, 1 dc in next st) 6 times. (12 sts)
Rnd 7: (dc2tog, 1 dc in next st) 4 times. (8 sts)
Stuff with fiberfill and continue stuffing as you go.
Rnds 8-15: 1 dc in each st. (8 sts)
Fasten off, leaving a long tail for sewing. Sew the feet to the bottom of the body on either sides of the body's magic ring.

## Hand and arm (make 2)

Using 2.75mm hook and col 2, make a magic ring.
Rnd 1 (RS): 6 dc into the magic ring. (6 sts)
Rnd 2: 2 dc in each st. (12 sts)
Rnd 3: (2 dc in next st, 1 dc in next st) 6 times. (18 sts)
Rnds 4-5: 1 dc in each st. (18 sts)
Rnd 6: (dc2tog, 1 dc in next st) 6 times. (12 sts)
Rnd 7: (dc2tog) 6 times. (6 sts)
Stuff with fiberfill and continue stuffing as you go.
Rnds 8-17: 1 dc in each st. (6 sts)
Fasten off, leaving a long tail for sewing. Sew the arms onto the body between the mouth and the top dark blue body line.

## Fingers

Using 2.75mm hook and col 2, attach your yarn onto one of the stitches on either side of the hand's magic ring. ch 2, work a 2 tr popcorn st in the same space. Turn your hook, and your work, so that you can dc back into the same stitch you started. Fasten off and weave in all yarn ends. Repeat this 3 more times.

## Attaching the eyes

With the yarn tail left over from making each eye you can now sew the eyes onto the head. Sew the entire back of the eye onto the body in a circle as this will be more secure. As you add more eyes they will begin to touch and you can sew the eye the ones adjacent to it, this will make the toy safer for young children. We recommend trying to keep two eyes the same size from being next to each other for a better final effect.

1

2

3

4

# Magical unicorn

Learn how to easily bring this much-loved fantasy creature into the real world – horn and all!

## Difficulty

★★☆☆☆

## What you need

- 2.75mm hook (US C/2)
- 9mm black safety eyes
- Yarn needle
- Fiberfill stuffing
- Scissors
- Stich marker (optional)
- You will need to use Aran weight yarn in your chosen colours. We have used Rosario 4 Catitano in:
  Colour 1: White (1 ball)
  Colour 2: Dark Pink (oddments)
  Colour 3: Grey (oddments)
  Colour 4: Yellow (oddments)
  Colour 5: Light pink (oddments)

## Measurements

28cm tall.

Designed by
**Mevlinn Gusick**

Mevlinn is a college graduate with a BFA in Fine Arts Painting. Her interest in knitting and crochet began when her aunt suggested she try knitting. It piqued her curiosity and here she is today, crocheting amigurumi whenever she gets the chance and giving them to those she loves.
www.mevvsan.com

## Pattern

### Body

Using col 1, make a magic ring.
Rnd 1 (RS): 7 dc in magic ring. (7 sts)
Rnd 2: 2 dc in each st around. (14 sts)
Rnd 3: (2 dc in next st, 1 dc in next st) 7 times. (21 sts)
Rnd 4: (2 dc in next st, 1 dc in next 2 sts) 7 times. (28 sts)
Rnd 5: (2 dc in next st, 1 dc in next 3 sts) 7 times. (35 sts)
Rnd 6: (2 dc in next st, 1 dc in next 4 sts) 7 times. (42 sts)
Rnd 7: 1 dc in each st around. (42 sts)
Rnd 8: (2 dc in next st, dc in next 5 sts) 7 times. (49 sts)
Rnd 9: 1 dc in each st around. (49 sts)
Rnds 10-12: dc2tog, 1 dc in each remaining st. (46 sts after rnd 12)
Rnds 13-14: dc2tog, 1 dc in each st to the last 3 sts, dc2tog, 1 dc in last st. (42 sts after rnd 14)
Stuff with fiberfill and continue stuffing as you go.
Rnds 15-22: dc2tog, 1 dc in each st to the last 3 sts, dc2tog, 1 dc in last st. (26 sts after rnd 22)
Rnds 23-28: dc2tog, 1 dc in each remaining st. (20 sts after rnd 28)
Fasten off leaving a tail for sewing. When the head is complete you will use this yarn end to sew the body and head together.
Note: The body has a side specific decrease. This decrease is creating the 'rump' of the unicorn. Keep this in mind when you sew the head on later.

### Head

Using col 1, make a magic ring.
Rnd 1 (RS): 6 dc in magic ring. (6 sts)
Rnd 2: 2 dc in each st around. (12 sts)
Rnd 3: (2 dc in next st, 1 dc in next st) 6 times. (18 sts)
Rnd 4: (2 dc in next st, 1 dc in next 2 sts) 6 times. (24 sts)
Rnd 5: (2 dc in next st, 1 dc in next 3 sts) 6 times. (30 sts)
Rnd 6: (2 dc in next st, 1 dc in next 4 sts) 6 times. (36 sts)
Rnds 7-15: 1 dc in each st around. (8 rnds of 36 sts)
Change to col 2.
Rnd 16: (2 dc in next st, 1 dc in next 5 sts) 6 times. (42 sts)
Place eyes between rnds 12 and 13 with 10 sts between the eyes.
Rnds 17-21: 1 dc in each st around. (5 rnds of 42 sts)
Stuff with fiberfill and continue stuffing as you go.
Rnd 22: (dc2tog, 1 dc in next 5 sts) 6 times. (36 sts)
Rnd 23: (dc2tog, 1 dc in next 4 sts) 6 times. (30 sts)
Rnd 24: (dc2tog, 1 dc in next 3 sts) 6 times. (24 sts)
Rnd 25: (dc2tog, 1 dc in next 2 sts) 6 times. (18 sts)
Rnd 26: (dc2tog, 1 dc in next st) 6 times. (12 sts)
Rnd 27: (dc2tog) 6 times. (6 sts)
Fasten off, leaving a long tail for sewing. Using your yarn needle, weave the yarn tail through the front ring of each remaining st and pull it tight to close. Sew head onto body. The back of the neck should sew onto rnd 6 of the head.

1

2

## Legs (make 2)

Using col 3, make a magic ring.
Rnd 1: 4 dc in magic ring. (4 sts)
Rnd 2: 2 dc in each st around. (8 sts)
Rnd 3: (2 dc in next st, 1 dc in next st) 4 times. (12 sts)
Rnd 4: 1 dc in each st around. (12 sts)
Change to col 1.
Rnd 5-17: 1 dc in each st around. (13 rounds of 12 sts)
Fasten off, leaving a tail for sewing.
Lightly stuff the legs with more stuffing near the hooves.

## Assemble the legs

Start by sewing the back legs first. Place the horse on a flat surface in the seated position that you will want it to be, and pin the legs to the sides of the body.
Attach the back legs at rnds 6-8 of the body with 12 sts between the initial attachment points of each leg. Sew each leg about 8 sts down the leg against the body to stop them from bowing out.
(See Fig. 1 & 2 on page 105.)
When the hind legs are attached, the unicorn should be able to sit well on its own, and this helps when sewing the front legs.
Attach the front legs at rnd 19 of the body with 4 sts between each leg. Sew each leg about 8 sts down the leg against the body to stop the front legs from bowing out.

## Ears (make 2)

Using col 1, ch 5.
Row 1: 1 dc in 2nd ch from hook, 1 dc in next 2 ch, 4 dc in last ch, rotate and work along the opposite side of the foundation ch, 1 dc in next 3 ch, turn. (10 sts)
Row 2: ch 1 (not counted as a st), 1 dc in next 3 sts, 2 dc in next 4 sts, 1 dc in next 3 sts, turn. (14 sts)
Row 3: ch 1 (not counted as a st), 1 dc in each st around. (14 sts)
Fasten off, leaving a tail for sewing. Pinch the base of the ear together and sew the ears 6 rnds behind the eyes with 9 sts between each ear.

## Horn

Using col 4, make a magic ring
Rnd 1 (RS): 4 dc in magic ring. (4 sts)
Rnds 2-6 (blo): 2 dc in next st, 1 dc in each remaining st. (9 sts after rnd 6)
Fasten off, leaving a long tail for sewing.
Sew the horn unstuffed onto the top of the head between the ears and the eyes.

## Tail

Cut 5 strands each of col 2 and col 5 that are 30 cm in length. Take one strand of each col and fold them in half. With the folded end between your fingers, insert your hook in the rump of your unicorn where you want the tail to be (about rnd 8 of the body), and place the folded ends of the yarn onto the hook and pull them back through the body. Take the loose ends of the yarn, wrap them around the hook and pull them through the ring. Pull to tighten. Repeat this 4 more times in sts adjacent to the first st to create a thick tail.
Separate the strands into 3 sections and braid or plait them. Take a piece of col 4 and wrap it around the end of the braid, then tie it tightly with a bow.

## Mane

Cut a few dozen strands each of cols 2 and 5 that are 25 cm in length. Find the centre of the unicorn's head and, using one strand at a time, attach the mane using the same method as given for the tail. To keep the mane straight, follow the sts down the back in a straight line until about 15 strands have been attached, alternating between col 2 and col 5. Repeat to add another line on each side of the centre mane to create 3 lines in total. Trim and braid or plait the mane if desired.

### Top Tip

Use different shades of the same colours to create a herd of unicorns to accompany your new friend, or use glittery yarn to give that added dash of magic.

# Flemish giant rabbit

Bring favourite characters or childhood pets to life by learning how to create a realistic rabbit

## Difficulty

★★★☆☆

## What you need

- 3mm hook (US D/3)
- Stitch marker
- Pair of 12mm black safety eyes
- Fiberfill
- Yarn needle
- Piece of Velcro, or a wire brush (optional)
- Embroidery floss and needle (optional)
- You will need DK yarn in your chosen colours.
  Colour 1: Body (1 ball)
  Colour 2: Tail (1 ball)

## Measurements

Body length: 22cm
Height (without ears): 10cm.

## Designed by Kati Gálusz

Kati is an amigurumi designer from Hungary. She loves to create patterns for realistic animals, and for her favourite movie and television characters. www.ravelry.com/designers/kati-galusz

## Pattern

### Front legs (make 2)

Using col 1 make a magic ring.
Rnd 1: 6 dc into magic ring, pull ring tight to close. (6 sts)
Rnd 2: 2 dc in each st. (12 sts)
Rnds 3-7: 1 dc in each st. ss into first st and fasten off.
(4 rnds of 12 sts)

### Head and body

Using col 1 make a magic ring.
Rnd 1: 6 dc into magic ring, pull ring tight to close. (6 sts)
Rnd 2: 2 dc in each st. (12 sts)
Rnd 3: (2 dc in next st, 1 dc in next st) 6 times. (18 sts)
Rnd 4: 1 dc in each st. (18 sts)
Rnd 5: (2 dc in next st, 1 dc in next 2 sts) 6 times. (24 sts)
Rnd 6: 1 dc in each st. (24 st)
Rnd 7: (2 dc in next st, 1 dc in next 3 sts) 6 times. (30 sts)
Rnds 8-9: 1 dc in each st.
(2 rnds of 30 sts)
Rnd 10: (2 dc in next st, 1 dc in next 4 sts) 6 times. (36 sts)
Rnds 11-13: 1 dc in each st.
(3 rnds of 36 sts)
Rnd 14: (1 dc in next st, 2 dc in next st) 3 times, 1 dc in next 7 sts, (2 dc in next st, dc in next 6 sts) 3 times, 1 dc in next 2 sts. (42 sts)
Rnd 15: (2 dc in next st, 1 dc in next 2 sts) 3 times, dc in next 33 sts. (45 sts)

The next round joins the front legs to the body.

Rnd 16: 1 dc in next st, then join as follows: hold a leg in front of the body and crochet through both layers, 1 dc in next 4 sts, continue working on the body only, 1 dc in next 3 sts, hold the second leg in front of the body and working through both layers, 1 dc in next 4 sts, continue on body only, 1 dc in next 33 sts. (45 sts)
Rnd 17: 1 dc in next st, then work as follows: Skip the 4 joining dc and instead work 1 dc in each of the 8 unworked leg sts from the last rnd, 1 dc in next 3 sts between the legs, skip the next 4 joining sts and work 1 dc in next 8 unworked sts of second leg, continuing on the body,
1 dc in next 13 sts, dc2tog, 1 dc in next 3 sts, dc2tog, 1 dc in next 13 sts. (51 sts)
Rnd 18: 2 dc in next st, 1 dc in next 7 sts, dc2tog, 1 dc in next st, dc2tog, 1 dc in next 7 sts,
2 dc in next st, 1 dc in next 14 sts, dc2tog, 1 dc in next 14 sts. (50 sts)
Rnd 19: 1 dc in next 32 sts, dc2tog, 1 dc in next 3 sts, dc2tog, 1 dc in next 11 sts. (48 sts)
Rnd 20: 1 dc in next 31 sts, dc2tog, 1 dc in next 3 sts, dc2tog, 1 dc in next 10 sts. (46 sts)
Rnd 21: 1 dc in next 33 sts, dc2tog, 1 dc in next 11 sts. (45 sts)
Stuff the head and front legs and place (do not fix) safety eyes between rnds 9 and 10, approx 12 sts apart. Remove stuffing then fix the eyes in place following manufacturer's instructions.
Rnds 22-28: 1 dc in each st.
(7 rnds of 45 sts)
Rnd 29: 1 dc in next 32 sts, (2 dc in next st, 1 dc in next 2 sts) 3 times, dc in next 4 sts. (48 sts)
Rnd 30: 1 dc in next 34 sts, 2 dc in next st, 1 dc in next 4 sts, 2 dc in next st, 1 dc in each of next 8 sts. (50 sts)
Rnds 31-32: 1 dc in each st.
Rnd 33: 1 dc in next 35 sts, 2 dc in next st, 1 dc in next 5 sts, 2 dc in next st, 1 dc in next 8 sts. (52 sts)

Rnds 34-35: 1 dc in each st.

Note: You need to start rnd 36 at the middle of the belly, so before continuing with rnd 36 make sure you work 1 dc in as many sts as necessary to be in the correct position (this will help to make the haunches symmetrical).

Rnd 36: 1 dc in next 6 sts, 2 dcflo in next 8 sts, 1 dc in next 24 sts, 2 dcflo in next 8 sts, 1 dc in next 6 sts. (68 sts)
Rnd 37: 1 dc in next 31 sts, 2 dc in next st, 1 dc in next 4 sts, 2 dc in next st, 1 dc in next 31 sts. (70 sts)
Rnd 38: 1 dc in next 7 sts, (dc2tog, 1 dc in next st) 5 times, 1 dc in next 26 sts, (1 dc in next st, dc2tog) 5 times, 1 dc in next 7 sts. (60 sts)
Rnds 39-43: 1 dc in each st. (5 rnds of 60 sts)
Stuff the head, front legs and shoulders.
Rnd 44: 1 dc in next 24 sts, (dc2tog, 1 dc in next 4 sts) 3 times, 1 dc in next 18 sts. (57 sts)
Rnds 45-46: 1 dc in each st. (2 rnds of 57 sts)
Rnd 47: 1 dc in next 24 sts, (dc2tog, 1 dc in next 3 sts) 3 times, 1 dc in next 18 sts. (54 sts)
Rnds 48-49: 1 dc in each st. (2 rnds of 54 sts)
Rnd 50: (1 dc in next 8 sts, dc2tog, 1 dc in next 8 sts) 3 times. (51 sts)
Rnd 51: (dc2tog, 1 dc in next 15 sts) 3 times. (48 sts)
Rnd 52: (1 dc in next 3 sts, dc2tog, 1 dc in next 3 sts) 6 times. (42 sts)
Rnd 53: (dc2tog, 1 dc in next 5 sts) 6 times. (36 sts)
Rnd 54: (1 dc in next 2 sts, dc2tog, 1 dc in next 2 sts) 6 times. (30 sts)
Rnd 55: (dc2tog, 1 dc in next 3 sts) 6 times. (24 sts)
Rnd 56: (1 dc in next st, dc2tog, 1 dc in next st) 6 times. (18 sts)

Start stuffing the body, making sure the stuffing is evenly distributed and emphasises the semi-arched backline.

Rnd 57: (dc2tog, 1 dc in next st) 6 times. (12 sts)
Add a little more toy filling if necessary.
Rnd 58: (dc2tog) 6 times. (6 sts) ss in next st, fasten off and use yarn end to close the remaining gap.

## Ears (make 2)

Using col 1, make a magic ring.
Rnd 1: 6 dc into magic ring, pull ring tight to close. (6 sts)
Rnd 2: (2 dc in next st, 1 dc in next 2 sts) twice. (8 sts)
Rnd 3: (2 dc in next st, 1 dc in next 3 sts) twice. (10 sts)
Rnd 4: (2 dc in next st, 1 dc in next 4 sts) twice. (12 sts)
Rnd 5: 1 dc in each st. (12 sts)
Rnd 6: (2 dc in next st, 1 dc in next 5 sts) twice. (14 sts)
Rnd 7: 1 dc in each st. (14 sts)
Rnd 8: (2 dc in next st, 1 dc in next 6 sts) twice. (16 sts)
Rnd 9: 1 dc in each st. (16 sts)
Rnd 10: (2 dc in next st, 1 dc in next 7 sts) twice. (18 sts)
Rnd 11: 1 dc in each st. (18 sts)
Rnd 12: (2 dc in next st, 1 dc in next 8 sts) twice. (20 sts)
Rnd 13: 1 dc in each st. (20 sts)
Rnd 14: (2 dc in next st, 1 dc in next 9 sts) twice. (22 sts)
Rnds 15-20: 1 dc in each st. (6 rnds of 22 sts)
ss into next st, fasten off leaving a long yarn end.
Flatten the ear, pinch together the bottom corners then sew them together to fix the ear in this position. Ears will define your bunny's personality. Sew them to the head in that position.

## Rear feet (make 2)

Using col 1, make a magic ring.
Rnd 1: 6 dc into magic ring, pull ring tight to close. (6 sts)
Rnd 2: 2 dc in each st. (12 sts)
Rnds 3-15: 1 dc in each st. (13 rnds or 12 sts)
Rnd 16: (dc2tog) 4 times, leaving remaining 4 sts unworked. (4 sts)
ss in next st and fasten off, leaving a long end.

Note: The rear feet bear no weight, so you can stuff them lightly.

Pin them to the body at ground level, just forward of the 'haunches'. Flatten the open ends to the body and sew to the body, then make a few sts between the body and feet about halfway forward so they stay in the right place.

## Tail

Using col 2, make a magic ring.
Rnd 1: 6 dc into magic ring, pull ring tight to close. (6 sts)
Rnd 2: 2 dc in each st. (12 sts)
Rnd 3: (2 dc in next st, 1 dc in next 3 sts) 3 times. (15 sts)
Rnds 4-7: 1 dc in each st. (2 rnds of 15 sts)
Rnd 8: (dc2tog, 1 dc in next 3 sts) 3 times. (12 sts)
Rnd 9: (dc2tog, 1 dc in next st) 4 times. (8 sts)
ss into next st, fasten off leaving a long end.
Stuff the tail lightly so it's rounded, but still flat. The closed tip of the tail should be placed where you closed the last rnd of the body. Flatten the bottom end of the tail then sew it to the body, closing the gap in the process. Then make a few sts between the body and tail to anchor it in the right position. If you want a fuzzy tail, brush the tail with a piece of Velcro or a wire brush until it becomes fluffy.

## Finishing

Using 6 strands of floss and a pointed embroidery needle, embroider the nose and the mouth.

## Top Tip

As you become more confident, try adding colour changes so you can replicate your beloved pet.

# Proud lion

Create your own pride of adorable lions with this simple but effective pattern that will have your lion sitting on his hind legs

### Difficulty

★★★☆☆

### What you need

- 3.75mm hook (US F/5)
- 1 pair 10mm oval safety eyes
- Yarn needle
- Fiberfill stuffing
- Pink and white felt
- Hot glue gun
- You will need to use DK weight yarn, in your chosen colours. We have used Bernat Handicrafter Cotton.
  Colour 1: Skin (2 balls)
  Colour 2: Paw (1 ball)
  Colour 3: Mane (1 ball)

### Measurements

21cm tall.

Designed by

**Amy Kember**

Amy is a technical writer living in Ottawa, Canada. Her interest in crochet began when she discovered an amigurumi book in a used bookstore. After making a pig, she was instantly hooked. Since 2010, Amy has been designing and selling her own amigurumi patterns on Etsy. www.etsy.com/shop/AmysGurumis

## Pattern

### Head

Using 3.75 mm hook and col 1, make a magic ring.
Rnd 1: 6 dc into ring and pull it closed. (6 sts)
Rnd 2: 2 dc in each dc. (12 sts)
Rnd 3: (1 dc in next dc, 2 dc in next dc) 6 times. (18 sts)
Rnd 4: (1 dc in each of next 2 dc, 2 dc in next dc) 6 times. (24 sts)
Rnd 5: (1 dc in each of next 3 dc, 2 dc in next dc) 6 times. (30 sts)
Rnd 6: (1 dc in each of next 4 dc, 2 dc in next dc) 6 times. (36 sts)
Rnd 7: (1 dc in each of next 5 dc, 2 dc in next dc) 6 times. (42 sts)
Rnd 8: (1 dc in each of next 6 dc, 2 dc in next dc) 6 times. (48 sts)
Rnds 9-16: 1 dc in each dc. (8 rnds of 48 sts)
Rnd 17: (1 dc in each of next 6 dc, dc2tog in next 2 dc) 6 times. (42 sts)
Rnd 18: (1 dc in each of next 5 dc, dc2tog in next 2 dc) 6 times. (36 sts)
Rnd 19: (1 dc in each of next 4 dc, dc2tog in next 2 dc) 6 times. (30 sts)
Rnd 20: (1 dc in each of next 3 dc, dc2tog in next 2 dc) 6 times. (24 sts)
Rnd 21: (1 dc in each of next 2 dc, dc2tog in next 2 dc) 6 times. (18 sts)
Rnd 22: (1 dc in next dc, dc2tog in next 2 dc) 6 times. (12 sts)
Fasten off.

### Body

Using col 1, make a magic ring.
Rnd 1: 6 dc into ring and pull it closed. (6 sts)
Rnd 2: 2 dc in each dc. (12 sts)
Rnd 3: (1 dc in next dc, 2 dc in next dc) 6 times. (18 sts)
Rnd 4: (1 dc in each of next 2 dc, 2 dc in next dc) 6 times. (24 sts)
Rnd 5: (1 dc in each of next 3 dc, 2 dc in next dc) 6 times. (30 sts)
Rnd 6: (1 dc in each of next 4 dc, 2 dc in next dc) 6 times. (36 sts)
Rnd 7: (1 dc in each of next 5 dc, 2 dc in next dc) 6 times. (42 sts)
Rnds 8-9: 1 dc in each dc. (2 rnds of 42 sts)
Rnd 10: (1 dc in each of next 5 dc, dc2tog in next 2 dc) 6 times. (36 sts)
Rnds 11-12: 1 dc in each dc. (2 rnds of 36 sts)
Rnd 13: (1 dc in each of next 4 dc, dc2tog in next 2 dc) 6 times. (30 sts)
Rnds 14-17: 1 dc in each dc. (4 rnds of 30 sts)
Rnd 18: (1 dc in each of next 3 dc, dc2tog in next 2 dc) 6 times. (24 sts)
Rnd 19: 1 dc in each dc. (24 sts)
Rnd 20: (1 dc in each of next 2 dc, dc2tog in next 2 dc) 6 times. (18 sts)
Fasten off.

### Ears (make 2)

Using col 1, make a magic ring.
Rnd 1: 6 dc into ring and pull it closed. (6 sts)
Rnds 2-4: 1 dc in each dc. (3 rnds of 6 sts)
Fasten off.

### Front legs (Make 2)

Using col 2, make a magic ring.
Rnd 1: 6 dc into ring and pull it closed. (6 sts)
Rnd 2: 2 dc in each dc. (12 sts)
Rnd 3: (1 dc in next dc, 2 dc in next dc) 6 times. (18 sts)
Rnd 4: 1 dc in each dc. (18 sts)
Rnd 5: (1 dc in next dc, dc2tog in next 2 dc) 6 times. (12 sts)
Change to col 1.

Rnd 6-11: 1 dc in each dc.
(6 rnds of 12 sts)
Rnd 12: (1 dc in next dc, dc2tog in next 2 dc)
4 times. (8 sts)
Rnds 13-17: 1 dc in each dc.
(5 rnds of 8 sts)
Fasten off.

## Back legs (Make 2)

Using col 2, make a magic ring.
Rnd 1: 6 dc into ring and pull it closed. (6 sts)
Rnd 2: 2 dc in each dc.
(12 sts)
Rnd 3: (1 dc in next dc, 2 dc in next dc) 6 times. (18 sts)
Rnd 4: 1 dc in each dc.
(18 sts)
Rnd 5: (1 dc in next dc, dc2tog in next 2 dc)
6 times. (12 sts)
Change to col 1.
Rnd 6-7: 1 dc in each dc.
(2 rnds of 12 sts)
Fasten off.

## Tail

Using col 3, make a magic ring.
Rnd 1: 6 dc into ring and pull it closed. (6 sts)
Rnd 2: 2 dc in each dc.
(12 sts)
Change to col 1.
Rnd 3: ch 16
Fasten off and weave in ends.

## Mane edging

Using col 3, ch 69.
Row 1: 1 dc into 2nd ch from hook, dc to end, turn. (48 sts)
Row 2: ch 3 (counts as tr), 4 tr in first dc, skip next dc, 1 ss in next dc, (skip next dc, 5 tr in next dc, skip next dc, 1 ss in next dc) 11 times, ss in last dc. (12 scallops made)
Fasten off.

## Mane

Using col 3, make a magic ring.
Rnd 1: 6 dc into ring and pull it closed. (6 sts)
Rnd 2: 2 dc in each dc.
(12 sts)
Rnd 3: (1 dc in next dc, 2 dc in next dc) 6 times. (18 sts)
Rnd 4: (1 dc in each of next 2 dc, 2 dc in next dc)
6 times. (24 sts)
Rnd 5: (1 dc in each of next 3 dc, 2 dc in next dc)
6 times. (30 sts)
Rnd 6: (1 dc in each of next 4 dc, 2 dc in next dc)
6 times. (36 sts)
Rnd 7: (1 dc in each of next 5 dc, 2 dc in next dc)
6 times. (42 sts)
Rnd 8: (1 dc in each of next 6 dc, 2 dc in next dc)
6 times. (48 sts)
Rnd 9-10: 1 dc in each dc.
(2 rnds of 48 sts)
Turn and begin working in rows.
Row 11: ch 1, 1 dc in each of next 42 dc, turn. (42 sts – leaving 6 dc unworked for the neck opening)
Rows 12-14: ch 1, 1 dc in each dc, turn. (3 rows of 42 sts)
Row 15 (make opening for ears): ch 1, 1 dc in each of next 11 dc, 6 ch, skip 5 dc, join in next dc with ss, 1 dc in each of next 8 dc, 6 ch, skip 5 dc, join in next dc with ss, 1 dc in each of next 11 dc, turn. (42 sts – do not count the slip sts from this rnd as sts in the following rnd)
Row 16: ch 1, dc in each dc. (42 sts)
Set aside while assembling the lion but do not fasten off.

## Assemble the face

Note: If you don't have a hot glue gun, you can always use fabric glue as an alternative. We recommend a hot glue gun as it's a stronger adhesive.

Insert 10 mm oval safety eyes between rnd 12 and rnd 13 of the head and position them 7 stitches apart. Stuff the head firmly.
Cut out a pink felt nose and a white felt mouth using the image as a guide.
Glue the nose to the mouth using a hot glue gun.
Position the mouth and nose between the eyes but slightly higher up on the face between rnd 10 and rnd 15.
Glue the mouth and nose to lion's face using a hot glue gun.

## Finishing

Stuff the body, arms, and legs.
Sew the body to the head – there is one extra decrease rnd on the head than on the body so the last rnd of the body (rnd 20) should be sewn around the second last rnd on the head (rnd 21).
Sew the arms to the body between rnd 16 and rnd 18 and position them so they are 4 stitches apart in the front.
Sew the legs to the body between rnd 7 and rnd 9 and position them 15 stitches apart in the front.

Note: As an optional extra, you could cut out two fabric inners for your lions ears, using hot glue to secure them in place.

Place the mane on Lion's head to determine the position of the ears (so they can poke through the ear openings in the mane).
Sew the ears to the head between rnd 5 and rnd 7.
To secure the mane, ch 6 across the neck and join on the other side of the mane with a slip stitch. Sew the mane edging to the mane.
Sew the tail to the back of the body between rnd 7 and rnd 8.

**Top Tip**

Create a pride of friends for your lion, leave the mane bonnet off to create some female friends.

# Yeti & bigfoot

With this pattern make a cute and cuddly monster; a snow-dwelling Yeti or a hairy mountain Bigfoot

### Difficulty

★★★☆☆

### What you need

- 3.5mm hook (US E/4)
- Pair of 15mm safety eyes
- Black yarn
- Fiberfill stuffing
- Wire pet brush
- Yarn needle
- In this project we have used Stylecraft Alpaca DK and Sirdar Country Style yarn in the following colours:
  Colour 1: Brown (Bigfoot)White (Yeti) (1 ball)
  Colour 2: Pale Pink (Bigfoot) Pale Blue (Yeti) (oddment)

### Measurements

23cm tall.

### Special stitches

Loop stitch: Insert your hook into the stitch, take the yarn under the hook and then over your middle or forefinger to make a loop. Make the loop about 2.5cm long, don't worry about making each one the same length. Pull the bottom of the loop (two strands) through. There are now 3 loops on the hook. You can pull the yarn to make the loop smaller if necessary. Yo, pull through all 3 loops.

6 tr pop stitch: ch 4 (counts as 1 tr) make 5 tr in same stitch. Remove your hook from the last st and insert it into the top of the starting ch 3. Insert your hook into the last st you made and pull through the top of the ch 3. ch 1 to close the stitch.

## Pattern

### Face (make this first)

Using col 2, ch2.
Rnd 1: 6 dc in 2nd ch from hook. (6 sts)
Rnd 2: 2 dc in each st around. (12 sts)
Rnd 3: (2 dc in next st, 1 dc in next st) 6 times. (18 sts)
Rnd 4: *1 dc in next 3 sts, (2 dc in next st, 1 dc in next st) 3 times; rep from * once more. (24 sts)
Rnd 5: 1 dc in next 4 sts, (2 dc in next st, 1 dc in next st) 3 times, 1 dc in next 6 sts, (2 dc in next st, 1 dc in next st) 3 times, 1 dc in next 2 sts. (30 sts).
Rnd 6: 1 dc in next 6 sts, (2 dc in next st, 1 dc in next st) 3 times, 1 dc in next 9 sts, (2 dc in next st, 1 dc in next st) 3 times, 1 dc in next 3 sts. (36 sts).
Rnd 7: 1 dc in next 6 sts, (2 dc in next st, 1 dc in next 2 sts) 3 times, 1 dc in next 9 sts, (2 dc in next st, 1 dc in next 2 sts) 3 times, 1 dc in next 3 sts. (42 sts)
Rnd 8: 1 dc in next 7 sts, (2 dc in next st, 1 dc in next 3 sts) 3 times, 1 dc in next 9 sts, (2 dc in next st, 1 dc in next 3 sts) 3 times, 1 dc in next 2 sts. (48 sts)
Change to col 1.
Rnd 9: 1 dc in each st around. (48 sts)
ss in next st, ch 1, turn to make ruff with the wrong side facing you.
Rnd 10: Loop stitch in each st around. (48 sts)
ss into first loop stitch and fasten off, leaving a long length of yarn to sew the face to the body. Next, cut the loops and using a wire pet brush, separate the strands of yarn to make them fuzzy. If you don't have a wire pet brush you can use a needle to separate the strands, it just takes a lot longer. Trim the ruff to the length you require.

### Embroider the mouth

Push the safety eyes through the face between rnds 5 and 6, on either side of the centre (do not attach the washers yet). Use the black yarn to embroider the mouth. Secure the end of the yarn on the back of the face before cutting yarn.

### Body

Using col 1, ch2.
Rnd 1: 6 dc in 2nd ch from hook. (6 sts)
Rnd 2: 2 dc in each st around. (12 sts)
Rnd 3: (2 dc in next st, 1 dc in next st) 6 times. (18 sts)

Designed by

## Lucy Collin

Lucy has been designing amigurumi for seven years. Her children encouraged her to use her crochet skills to make them cute toys, and she then started to sell the patterns online. She has had two books published, including Star Wars Crochet. lucyravenscar.blogspot.com

Rnd 4: (2 dc in next st, 1 dc in next 2 sts) 6 times. (24 sts)
Rnd 5: (2 dc in next st, 1 dc in next 3 sts) 6 times. (30 sts)
Rnd 6: (2 dc in next st, 1 dc in next 4 sts) 6 times. (36 sts)
Rnd 7: (2 dc in next st, 1 dc in next 5 sts) 6 times.
(42 sts)
Rnd 8: (2 dc in next st, 1 dc in next 6 sts) 6 times.
(48 sts)
Rnd 9: (2 dc in next st, 1 dc in next 7 sts) 6 times.
(54 sts)
Rnd 10: (2 dc in next st, 1 dc in next 8 sts) 6 times. (60 sts)
Rnds 11-30: 1 dc in each st around. (20 rnds of 60 sts)
Rnd 31: (2 dc in next st, 1 dc in next 9 sts) 6 times. (66 sts)
Rnd 32: 1 dc in each st around. (66 sts)
Rnd 33: (2 dc in next st, 1 dc in next 10 sts) 6 times. (72 sts)
Rnd 34: 1 dc in each st around. (72 sts)
Rnd 35: (2 dc in next st, 1 dc in next 11 sts) 6 times. (78 sts)
Rnds 36-55: 1 dc in each st around. (20 rnds of 78 sts)
Put the start of the current round at the back. Then fit the face to the body by pushing the safety eyes through both the face and the body, before fitting the washers on the inside. As a guide, the top of the face, not including the ruff, should be level with rnd 10, which means the eyes should be fixed between rnds 19 and 20 of the body.
Stuff the body firmly and continue to stuff as you work the next few rounds.
Rnd 56: (dc2tog, 1 dc in next 11 sts) 6 times. (72 sts)
Rnd 57: (dc2tog, 1 dc in next 10 sts) 6 times. (66 sts)
Rnd 58: (dc2tog, 1 dc in next 9 sts) 6 times. (60 sts)
Rnd 59: (dc2tog, 1 dc in next 8 sts) 6 times. (54 sts)
Rnd 60: (dc2tog, 1 dc in next 7 sts) 6 times. (48 sts)
Rnd 61: (dc2tog, 1 dc in next 6 sts) 6 times. (42 sts)
Rnd 62: (dc2tog, 1 dc in next 5 sts) 6 times. (36 sts)
Rnd 63: (dc2tog, 1 dc in next 4 sts) 6 times. (30 sts)
Rnd 64: (dc2tog, 1 dc in next 3 sts) 6 times. (24 sts)
Rnd 65: (dc2tog, 1 dc in next 2 sts) 6 times. (18 sts)
Rnd 66: (dc2tog, 1 dc in next st) 6 times. (12 sts)
Rnd 67: (dc2tog) 6 times.
(6 sts)
Fasten off, leaving a tail.
Finish stuffing firmly then sew up hole at bottom. Pull the yarn upwards through the body to make the bottom a bit more flat, then pass the yarn through the body a couple of times before cutting.
Sew the face to the body using the length of col 1 that you left attached after making the ruff. As you sew it, make sure you hide the tops of the loop stitches behind the face.

## Legs (make 2)

Using col 2, ch2.
Rnd 1: 6 dc in 2nd ch from hook. (6 sts)
Rnd 2: 2 dc in each st around. (12 sts)
Rnd 3: 2 dc in each st around. (24 sts)
Rnd 4: (2 dc in next st, 1 dc in next 3 sts) 6 times.
(30 sts)
Rnd 5: (2 dc in next st, 1 dc in next 4 sts) 6 times.
(36 sts)
Rnd 6: (2 dc in next st, 1 dc in next 5 sts) 6 times.
(42 sts)
Rnd 7: (2 dc in next st, 1 dc in next 6 sts) 6 times.
(48 sts)
Rnd 8: 1 dc in next 15 sts, (6 tr pop over next 2 sts, 1 dc in next st) 6 times, 1 dc in next 15 sts. (42 sts)
Rnd 9-10: 1 dc in each st around. (2 rnds of 42 sts)
Change to col 1.
Rnd 11: (dc2tog, 1 dc in next 5 sts) 6 times. (36 sts)
Rnd 12-15: 1 dc in each st around. (4 rnds of 36 sts)
Rnd 16: (dc2tog, 1 dc in next 4 sts) 6 times. (30 sts)
Rnd 17-20: 1 dc in each st around. (4 rnds of 30 sts)
Rnd 21: (dc2tog, 1 dc in next 3 sts) 6 times. (24 sts)
Rnd 22-25: 1 dc in each st around. (4 rnds of 24 sts)
ss in next st and fasten off, leaving a long length of yarn.

Stuff the legs, then sew them to the bottom of the body.

## Left arm

Using col 2, ch 17 loosely (if necessary use a 4mm hook just for the chain), 1 dc in 2nd ch from hook, (6tr pop over next 2 ch, 1 dc in next ch) 5 times. (11 sts)

Rnd 1: (Place stitch marker before first dc) 1 dc into the back of next 16 ch, then work into the top of the popcorn stitches and dc as follows: 1 dc in next st, (1 dc in next st, 2 dc in next st) 5 times. (32 sts)

Rnds 2-3: 1 dc in each st around. (2 rnds of 32 sts)

Rnd 4: 1 dc in next 15 sts, 6 tr pop over next 2 sts, 1 dc in next 15 sts. (31 sts)

## Right arm:

Rep rnds 1-3 of left arm.

Rnd 4: 6 tr pop over next 2 sts, 1 dc in next 30 sts. (31 sts)

Change to col 1.

Rnd 5: 1 dc in each st around. (31 sts)

Rnd 6: dc2tog, 1 dc in next 29 sts. (30 sts)

Rnd 7: 1 dc in each st around. (30 sts)

Rnd 8: (dc2tog, 1 dc in next 8 sts) 3 times. (27 sts)

Rnds 9-10: 1 dc in each st around. (2 rnds of 27 sts)

Rnd 11: (dc2tog, 1 dc in next 7 sts) 3 times. (24 sts)

Rnd 12-13: 1 dc in each st around. (2 rnds of 24 sts)

Rnd 14: (dc2tog, 1 dc in next 6 sts) 3 times. (21 sts)

Rnd 15-19: 1 dc in each st around. (5 rnds of 21 sts)

Rnd 20: (dc2tog, 1 dc in next 5 sts) 3 times. (18 sts)

Rnds 21-27: 1 dc in each st around. (7 rnds of 18 sts)

Rnd 28: (dc2tog, 1 dc in next 4 sts) 3 times. (15 sts)

Rnd 29-35: 1 dc in each st around. (7 rnds of 15 sts)

Stuff each arm, more firmly at the finger end, less towards the top.

Rnd 36: (dc2tog, 1 dc in next 3 sts) 3 times. (12 sts)

Rnd 37: (dc2tog, 1 dc in next 4 sts) twice. (10 sts)

ss into next st and fasten off, leaving a long length of yarn.

Sew arms to either side of the body a little higher than the bottom of the face, about level with the top of rnd 24 of the body.

# Pearl the dolphin

Requiring only basic stitches and less than 70g of yarn, Pearl is a quick and cute amigurumi that can take shape in just an afternoon!

## Difficulty

★★☆☆☆

## What you need

- 5mm hook (US H/8)
- Pair of 9mm safety eyes
- Fiberfill stuffing
- Scissors
- Stitch markers
- Yarn needle
- You will need to use Aran weight yarn in your chosen colours. We have used Lion Brand Vanna's Choice in:
  Colour 1: Sky blue (1 ball)
  Colour 2: White (1 ball)

## Measurements

11.5 cm long, 7.5 cm tall.

Designed by

## Sarah Sloyer

When Sarah first discovered amigurumi, she became determined to teach herself how to crochet so she could make them! After lots of practice, she is finally designing and writing her own patterns, which she loves sharing with others. www.ravelry.com/stores/critterbeans.

## Pattern

### Body

Using col 1, ch 8.

Rnd 1: 1 dc in 2nd ch from hook, 1 dc in next 5 ch, 4 dc in next ch, rotate and work along the opposite side of foundation chain, 1 dc in next 5 ch, 4 dc in last ch. You will now have a small oval shape. Place stitch marker in next st (this is be the first st of next round). (19 sts)

Rnd 2: 1 dc in next 7 sts, 3 dc in next st, 2 dc in next st, 1 dc in next 7 sts, 3 dc in next st, 2 dc in next st, 1 dc in last st (25 sts)

Rnd 3: 1 dc in next 8 sts, 2 dc in next 3 sts, 1 dc in next 10 sts, 2 dc in next 3 sts, 1 dc in next st. (31 sts)

Rnd 4: 1 dc in next 7 sts,
(2 dc in next st, 1 dc in next st) 5 times, 1 dc in next 9 sts, 2 dc in next 3 sts, 1 dc in next 2 sts. (39 sts)

Rnd 5: 1 dc in each st around. (39 sts)

Rnd 6: 1 dc in next 33 sts, 2 dc in next 3 sts, 1 dc in next 3 sts. (42 sts)

Rnd 7: 1 dc in each st around. (42 sts)

Rnd 8: 1 dc in next 10 sts, (2 dc in next st, 1 dc in next 2 sts)
4 times, 1 dc in next 13 sts, 2 dc in next 3 sts, 1 dc in next 4 sts. (49 sts)

Rnd 9: 1 dc in each st around. (49 sts)

Rnd 10: 1 dc in next 40 sts,
2 dc in next 3 sts, 1 dc in next
6 sts. (52 sts)

Rnd 11: 1 dc in next 15 sts, 2 dc in next 5 sts, 1 dc in next 32 sts. (57 sts)

Note: On rnds 11 and 12, the stitches that form the dolphin's nose are very tight because of the multiple increases packed closely together from the previous rounds. It may be hard to see and work into these stitches; take your time so that you don't miss any.

Rnd 12: 1 dc in next 18 sts, 2 dc in next 4 sts, 1 dc in next 25 sts, 2 dc in next 3 sts, 1 dc in next
7 sts. (64 sts)

Rnd 13: 1 dc in each st around. (64 sts)

Note: Rnds 13, 14 and 15 are all shaped using lots of unevenly spaced decreases. Keep track of your stitches as you go by crossing stitches off.

Rnd 14: 1 dc in next st, dc2tog, 1 dc in next 5 sts, dc2tog, 1 dc in next 7 sts, (dc2tog) 5 times,
1 dc in next 7 sts, dc2tog, 1 dc in next 6 sts, dc2tog, 1 dc in next 8 sts, dc2tog, 1 dc in next st, dc2tog, 1 dc in next 6 sts,
1 dc in last st changing to col 2. (53 sts)

Rnd 15: 1 dc in next st, dc2tog, 1 dc in next 5 sts, dc2tog, 1 dc in next 4 sts, (dc2tog) 4 times,
1 dc in next 4 sts, dc2tog, 1 dc in next 5 sts, dc2tog, 1 dc in next 8 sts, (dc2tog) twice, 1 dc in next 6 sts. (43 sts)

Rnd 16: dc2tog, 1 dc in next
5 sts, dc2tog, 1 dc in next
4 sts, dc2tog, 1 dc in next 4 sts, dc2tog, 1 dc in next 5 sts, dc2tog, 1 dc in next 5 sts, dc2tog, 1 dc in next st, dc2tog, 1 dc in next

5 sts. (36 sts)
Rnd 17: 1 dc in next 2 sts, dc2tog, (1 dc in next 4 sts, dc2tog) 5 times, 1 dc in next 2 sts. (30 sts)
Next, fix eyes as follows: count 3 rounds up from where col 2 starts. Starting at the tip of the nose, count 10 stitches away on either side and place each eye with 18 stitches between them.

Rnd 18: (1 dc in next 3 sts, dc2tog) 6 times. (24 sts)
Rnd 19: 1 dc in next st, dc2tog, (1 dc in next 2 sts, dc2tog)
5 times, 1 dc in next st. (18 sts)
Begin stuffing the body firmly. Poke the stuffing into the nose to fill in its shape, and towards the sides of the dolphin's body, until the decreases made in the previous rounds are less prominent and the body is rounder.

Rnd 20: (1 dc in next st, dc2tog) 6 times. (12 sts)
Continue stuffing the body as you complete the final rounds. You can use the blunt end of your hook to push the stuffing up into the body.
Rnd 21: (dc2tog) 6 times.
(6 sts)
Cut yarn and fasten off leaving a long tail. Thread yarn tail through the front rings of the remaining 6 sts then pull tight to gather.

## Tail fins (make 2)

In col 1, make a magic ring.
Rnd 1 (RS): 6 dc in magic ring. (6 sts)
Rnd 2: (1 dc in next 2 sts, 2 dc in next st) twice. (8 sts)
Rnd 3: 1 dc in each st around. (8 sts)
Rnd 4: (1 dc in next 3 sts, 2 dc in next st) twice. (10 sts)
Rnd 5: 1 dc in each st around. (10 sts)

When you have completed the first fin, fasten off.
When you have completed the second fin, do not fasten off.

Join the two fins together as follows: with your working yarn (and second fin) still on your hook, insert hook into the first stitch of the first fin. Yarn over and pull through a slip stitch. ch 1, dc around both fins, creating one piece.
When you have double crocheted around once, fasten off with a slip stitch. Do not stuff; press flat and set aside for assembly.

### Dorsal fin

In col 1, make a magic ring.
Rnd 1 (RS): 6 dc in magic ring. (6 sts).
Rnd 2: 1 dc in each st around. (6 sts)
Rnd 3: 2 dc in next 3 sts, 1 dc in next 3 sts. (9 sts)
Rnd 4: 1 dc in each st around. (9 sts)
Rnd 5: 1 dc in next 2 sts, 2 dc in next 2 st, 1 dc in next 5 sts. (11 sts)
Fasten off and leave a long tail for sewing. Do not stuff; press flat and set aside for assembly.
(See Fig. 1-3)

### Side fins (make 2)

In col 1, make a magic ring.
Rnd 1 (RS): 6 dc in magic ring. (6 sts).
Rnd 2: 1 dc in each st around. (6 sts)
Rnd 3: (1 dc in next st, 2 dc in next st) 3 times. (9 sts)
Rnd 4: 1 dc in each st around. (9 sts)
Do not fasten off or stuff; press flat and dc across the top of the fin, through both sides, to close. Fasten off, leaving a tail for sewing.

## Finishing

### Dorsal fin

With the top fin pressed flat, place and pin to the body with your yarn tail facing the front of the body. This ensures that the increases you made in rnds 2 and 4 of the top fin are facing the back of the dolphin, giving the fin its curved appearance.

### Side fins

The side fins are sewn into the round directly above where the body changes from col 1 to col 2. (See Fig. 5-6)

### Tail

Pin and sew tail to body using Fig 4. as a guide.

Shade no:
Shade colour:
Lot: 1370
THE
WOMEN'
INSTITUT

# Baby guinea pigs

Quick to make and using minimal amounts of yarn, these little cuties would be perfect for last-minute gifts or party favours

### Difficulty

★★★☆☆

### What you need

- 3mm hook (US D/3)
- Stitch marker
- Pair of 7.5mm black safety eyes
- Fiberfill stuffing
- Yarn needle
- Wire cutter (optional)
- You will need DK weight yarn in your chosen colours. We have used Red Heart yarn

### Measurements

Length: 5.5-6cm
Height: 3.5-4cm

### Special stitches

4tr-bobble: *yo, insert hook into st, yo and draw up a loop, yo and pull through two loops on hook.* Rep from * to * 3 times in same stitch. Yo and pull through 5 loops on hooks.

Designed by
**Kati Gálusz**

Kati is an amigurumi designer from Hungary. She loves to create patterns for realistic animals, and for her favourite movie and television characters. www.ravelry.com/designers/kati-galusz

## Pattern

### Beige guinea pig

Colour 1: Beige (oddments)
Colour 2: Pink (oddments)

### Head and body

Using col 1 make a magic ring.
Rnd 1: 6 dc in magic ring, pull ring tight to close. (6 sts)
Rnd 2: (2 dc in next st, 1 dc in next st) 3 times. (9 sts)
Rnd 3: (2 dc in next st, 1 dc in next st) 3 times, 1 dc in next 3 sts. (12 sts)
Rnd 4: (2 dc in next st, 1 dc in next 2 sts) 3 times, 1 dc in next 3 sts. (15 sts)
Rnd 5: 1 dc in each st around. (15 sts)
Rnd 6: 1 dc in next 5 sts, 2 dc in next st, 1 dc in next 5 sts, 2 dc in next st, 1 dc in next 2 sts, 2 dc in next st. (18 sts)
Rnd 7: 1 dc in next 13 sts, 2 dc in next st, 1 dc in next 2 sts, 2 dc in next st, 1 dc in next st. (20 sts)
Rnd 8: 1 dc in next 14 sts, 4tr-bobble in next st, 1 dc in next 2 sts, 4tr-bobble in next st, 1 dc in next 2 sts. (20 sts)
Rnd 9: 1 dc in next 5 sts, dc2tog, 1 dc in next 13 sts. (19 sts)
Rnd 10: 1 dc in each st around. (19 sts)

Next, insert safety eyes between rnds 4 and 5 on either side of the head, 6-7 stitches apart. If the eye stems are too long for the tiny head, use a wire cutter to chop off a few mm so they fit in comfortably. Stuff head, making sure that stuffing gets all the way to the nose, beyond the eye stems.

Rnd 11: 1 dc in next 6 sts, 2 dc in next st, 1 dc in next 12 sts. (20 sts)
Rnd 12: 1 dc in each st around. (20 sts)
Rnd 13: 1 dc in next 4 sts, dc2tog, 1 dc in next 2 sts, dc2tog, 1 dc in next 10 sts. (18 sts)
Rnd 14: 1 dc in next 3 sts, dc2tog, 1 dc in next 2 sts, dc2tog, 1 dc in next 9 sts. (16 sts)
Rnd 15: (Invdec, 1 dc in next 2 sts) 4 times. (12 sts)
Stuff body firmly.
Rnd 16: (Invdec) 6 times. (6 sts)

Before fastening off, check that your guinea pig can sit. If it falls on its nose, try pushing a little more stuffing into the bottom, and pull the bobble stitches outwards so the front legs stick out more.
Once you are happy with your guinea, fasten off and use yarn end to close the remaining hole.

### Ears (make 2)

Using col 2, make a magic ring.
Rnd 1: ch 2, (1 htr, 2 dc, 1 htr) into the ring, ch 2, ss into the ring. Cut yarn leaving a long end, and fasten off. Pull to close the ring.
Sew the ears to the head: they should lay flat on the head and nearly touch the eyes.

### Rear feet (make 2)

Using col 1, ch 5.
Row 1: 1 dc in second ch from hook and in the next 3 ch, turn. (4 sts)
Row 2: ch 1 (not counted as a st), 1 dc in

each st to end, turn. (4 sts)
Row 3: ch 1, fold the piece in half lengthwise and line up the free edge of the beginning chain with the stitches of Row 2. Working through both layers, ss in next 4 sts. Fasten off, leaving a long yarn end.

### Finishing

Place the legs beside the body – the tips should be 1-2 rnds behind the front legs, with yarn tails near the bottom. Sew this end to the guinea pig then make a few stitches at the middle of the leg to anchor it safely to the body.

## Pattern
### Brown and tan guinea pig

Colour 1: Brown (oddments)
Colour 2: Tan (oddments)

### Head and body

Using col 1, follow instructions as for the beige guinea pig for rnds 1-7.
Rnd 8: 1 dc in next 14 sts, 4tr-bobble, 1 dc in next st, change to col 2, 1 dc in next st, 4tr-bobble in next st, 1 dc in next 2 sts. (20 sts)
Rnd 9: 1 dc in next 4 sts, change to col 1, 1 dc in next st, dc2tog, 1 dc in next 7 sts, change to col 2, 1 dc in next 6 sts. (19 sts)
Rnd 10: 1 dc in next 7 sts, change to col 1, 1 dc in next 5 sts, change to col 2, 1 dc in next 7 sts (19 sts)
Insert safety eyes between rnds 4 and 5 on either side of the head, 6-7 stitches apart. If the eye stems are too long for the tiny head, use a wire cutter to chop off a few mm so they fit in comfortably. Stuff head, making sure that stuffing gets all the way to the nose, beyond the eye stems.

Rnd 11: 1 dc in next 6 sts,
2 dc in next st, 1 dc in next st, change to col 1, 1 dc in next 3 sts, change to col 2, 1 dc in next 8 sts. (20 sts)
Rnd 12: 1 dc in next 9 sts, change to col 1, 1 dc in next 2 sts, change to col 2, 1 dc in next 9 sts. (20 sts)
Rnd 13: 1 dc in next 4 sts, dc2tog, 1 dc in next 2 sts, dc2tog, 1 dc in next 10 sts. (18 sts)
Rnd 14: 1 dc in next 3 sts, dc2tog, 1 dc in next 2 sts, dc2tog, 1 dc in next 2 sts, change to col 1, 1 dc in next 7 sts. (16 sts)
Rnds 15-16: Using col 1, follow the instructions given for the beige guinea pig.

### Ears and rear feet

Using col 1, follow instructions given for the beige guinea pig.

## Pattern
### Grey and white guinea pig

Colour 1: Grey (oddments)
Colour 2: White (oddments)

### Head and body

Using col 2 make a magic ring.
Rnd 1 (RS): 6 dc in magic ring, pull ring tight to close. (6 sts)
Rnd 2: 2 dc in next st, 1 dc in next st, change to col 1,
(2 dc in next st, 1 dc in next st) twice. (9 sts)
Rnd 3: 2 dc in next st, change to col 2, 1 dc in next st, 2 dc in next st, change to col 1, 1 dc in next st, 2 dc in next st, 1 dc in next 4 sts. (12 sts)
Rnd 4: 2 dc in next st, 1 dc in next st, change to col 2, 1 dc in next st, 2 dc in next st, 1 dc in next st, change to col 1, 1 dc in next st, 2 dc in next st, 1 dc in next 5 sts. (15 sts)
Rnd 5: 1 dc in next 3 sts, change to col 2, 1 dc in next 4 sts, change to col 1, 1 dc in next 8 sts. (15 sts)
Rnd 6: 1 dc in next 4 sts, change to col 2, 1 dc in next st, 2 dc in next st, change to col 1, 1 dc in next 5 sts, 2 dc in next st, 1 dc in next 2 sts, 2 dc in next st. (18 sts)
Rnds 7-16: Follow instructions given for the beige guinea pig in col 2.

### Ears and rear feet

Follow instructions given for the beige guinea pig using col 1 for each piece.

# Pattern
## Tricolour guinea pig

Colour 1: Chestnut (oddments)
Colour 2: White (oddments)
Colour 3: Black (oddments)

### Head and body

Rnds 1-7: Follow instructions given for the beige guinea pig. (20 sts)
Rnd 8: 1 dc in next 6 sts, change to col 2, 1 dc in next
8 sts, 4tr-bobble in next st, 1 dc in next 2 sts, 4tr-bobble in next st, 1 dc in next 2 sts.
Rnd 9: 1 dc in next 5 sts, dc2tog, 1 dc in next 13 sts.
(19 sts)
Rnd 10: 1 dc in each st around. (19 sts).
Insert safety eyes between rnds 4 and 5 on either side of the head, 6-7 stitches apart. If the eye stems are too long for the tiny head, use a wire cutter to chop off a few mm so they fit in comfortably. Stuff head, making sure that stuffing gets all the way to the nose, beyond the eye stems.

Rnd 11: 1 dc in next 4 sts, change to col 3, 1 dc in next
2 sts, 2 dc in next st, 1 dc in next 5 sts, change to col
2, 1 dc in next 7 sts. (20 sts)
Rnd 12: 1 dc in next 2 sts, change to col 3, 1 dc in next
18 sts. (20 sts)
Rnd 13: 1 dc in next 4 sts, dc2tog, 1 dc in next 2 sts, dc2tog, 1 dc in next 10 sts.
(18 sts)
Rnd 14: Change to col 1, 1 dc in next 3 sts, dc2tog, 1 dc in next st, change to col 3, 1 dc in next st, dc2tog, 1 dc in next 5 sts, change to col 1, 1 dc in next 4 sts. (16 sts)
Rnds 15-16: Follow instructions given for the beige guinea pig.

### Ears

Using col 1 follow instructions given for the beige guinea pig.

### Rear feet

Follow instructions given for the beige guinea pig using col 1 for one foot and col 3 for the other. Attach each foot to the side where its col is the more dominant.

# Pattern
## White and brown guinea pig

Colour 1: White (oddments)
Colour 2: Light Brown (oddments)

### Head and body

Using col 1 make a magic ring.
Rnd 1 (RS): 6 dc in magic ring, pull ring tight to close. (6 sts)
Rnd 2: (2 dc in next st, 1 dc in next st) twice, 2 dc in next st, change to col 2, 1 dc in next st.
(9 sts)
Rnd 3: 1 dc in next st, 2 dc in next st, change to col 1, 1 dc in next st, change to col 2, 2 dc in next st, 1 dc in next 2 sts, change to col 1, 2 dc in next st, 1 dc in next st, change to col 2, 1 dc in next st. (12 sts)
Rnd 4: 2 dc in next st, 1 dc in next 2 sts, change to col 1, 2 dc in next st, change to col 2, 1 dc in next 2 sts, 2 dc in next st, 1 dc in next st, change to col 1, 1 dc in next 3 sts, change to col 2, 1 dc in next st. (15 sts)
Rnd 5: 1 dc in next 4 sts, change to col 1, 1 dc in next 2 sts, change to col 2, 1 dc in next 5 sts, change to col 1, 1 dc in next 3 sts, change to col
2, 1 dc in next st. (15 sts)
Rnd 6: 1 dc in next 4 sts, change to col 1, 1 dc in next st, 2 dc in next st, change to col
2, 1 dc in next 5 sts, change to col 1, 2 dc in next st, 1 dc in next 3 sts, change to col
2, 1 dc in the same st as previous dc. (18 sts)
Rnd 7: 1 dc in next 3 sts, change to col 1, 1 dc in next 5 sts, change to col 2, 1 dc in next 4 sts, change to col 1,
(1 dc in next st, 2 dc in next st,
1 dc in next st) twice. (20 sts)
Rnds 8-16: Follow the instructions given for the beige guinea pig

### Ears and rear feet

Follow instructions given for the beige guinea pig in col 1.

# Tiny luck elephant

Tiny luck elephant is a preciously petite project that is quick and easy to make and is the perfect gift for a child

## Difficulty

★★☆☆☆

## What you need

- 3.25mm hook (US D/3)
- 1 pair 6mm safety eyes
- Cotton fabric
- Yarn needles
- Fiberfill stuffing
- Two stitch markers
- Embroidery thread
- You will need super DK weight yarn in your chosen colours. We have used BBB filati Full: 100% pure new wool.
  Colour 1: Elephant (1 ball)
  Colour 2: Flower (oddment)

## Measurements

9cm in sitting position.

## Designed by Mari-Liis Lille

Mari-Liis known as lilleliis has been crazy about amigurumi since 2008 when she first discovered crochet. Since then designing toys has become her greatest passion and self-realisation. She is the author of many pattern books published in her native language Estonian as well as in English, Dutch, Korean and Spanish. www.lilleliis.com

## Pattern

### Head

Using 3.25mm hook and col 1, make a magic ring.

Rnd 1: 6 dc into ring and pull it closed. (6 sts)

Rnd 2: 1 dc in each dc. (6 sts)

Rnd 3: 1 dc in each of next 2 dc, 2 dc in next dc, 1 dc in each of next 3 dc. (7 sts)

Rnd 4: 1 dc in each of next 2 dc, 2 dc in next dc, 1 dc in each of next 4 dc. (8 sts)

Rnd 5: 1 dc in each of next 2 dc, 2 dc in next dc, 1 dc in each of next 5 dc. (9 sts)

Rnd 6: 1 dc in each of next 2 dc, 2 dc in next dc, 1 dc in each of next 6 dc. (10 sts)

Rnd 7: 1 dc in each of next 2 dc, 2 dc in next dc, 1 dc in each of next 7 dc. (11 sts)

Rnd 8: 1 dc in each of next 2 dc, 2 dc in next dc, 1 dc in each of next 8 dc. (12 sts)

Rnd 9: 1 dc in each of next 2 dc, 2 dc in each of next 2 dc, 1 dc in each of next 8 dc. (14 sts)

Rnd 10: (1 dc in each of next 2 dc, 2 dc in next dc) twice, 1 dc in each of next 8 dc. (16 sts)

Rnd 11: 1 dc in next dc, 2 dc in next dc, 1 dc in each of next 8 dc, 2 dc in next dc, 1 dc in each of next 5 dc. (18 sts)

Mark the first stitch of the next round with your marker and do not move it from there as you will need it when placing the safety eyes. You can mark the beginning of the coming rounds with the second stitch marker.

Rnd 12: (1 dc in next dc, 2 dc in next dc) 6 times, 1 dc in each of next 6 dc. (24 sts)

Rnd 13: (1 dc in each of next 3 dc, 2 dc in the next dc) 6 times. (30 sts)

Rnds 14-18: 1 dc in each dc, do not fasten off.
(5 rnds of 30 sts)

Go back to rnd 12 where you have the first stitch marked. Find the second increase in this row (the stitch where you've made 2 dc in one st) and insert the safety eye right below it. Insert the second eye below the 5th increase. You should see 5 stitches between the two eyes. Close the washers on the inside of the work.

Rnd 19: (1 dc in each of next 3 dc, dc2tog) 6 times. (24 sts)

Rnd 20: 1 dc in each dc. (24 sts)

Stuff the trunk and continue adding stuffing.

Rnd 21: (1 dc in each of next 2 dc, dc2tog) 6 times. (18 sts)

Rnd 22: 1 dc in each dc. (18 sts)

Rnd 23: (1 dc in next dc, dc2tog) 6 times. (12 sts)

Rnd 24: (dc2tog) 6 times. (6 sts).

Fasten off leaving a tail for closing the piece. Hook yarn through the front loops of all 6 sts on the last round and pull tight. Make a knot and weave in yarn end.

### Ears (make 2)

Using col 1, make a magic ring.

Rnd 1: 6 dc into ring and pull it closed. (6 sts)

Rnd 2: Work 2 dc in each dc. (12 sts)

Rnd 3: (1 dc in next dc, 2 dc in next dc) 6 times. (18 sts)

Rnd 4: (1 dc in each of next 2 dc, 2 dc in next dc) 6 times. (24 sts)

Rnd 5: (1 dc in each of next 3 dc, 2 dc in next dc) 6 times. (30 sts)

Rnd 6: 1 dc in each dc. (30 sts)

Fold the piece in half keeping your hook at the right corner. Crochet along the open edge working through both layers. Work 15 dc along the edge.

Fasten off, leaving a long tail for sewing.

### Assembling the ears

The ears need to mirror each another and

are attached from above, so bring the yarn tail of one of the ears out on the other tip of the ear.
Cut out pieces of fabric following the shape of the ears. Sew them on. Attach the ears to the head. Make only a half seam from the top to the middle of the ear (the place where you can see the starting magic ring).
Stitch eyelashes.

## Body

Using col 1, make a magic ring.
Rnd 1: 6 dc into ring and pull it closed. (6 sts)
Rnd 2: 2 dc in each dc around. (12 sts)
Rnd 3: (1 dc in next dc, 2 dc in next dc) 6 times. (18 sts)
Rnd 4: (1 dc in each of next 2 dc, 2 dc in next dc) 6 times. (24 sts)
Rnds 5-7: 1 dc in each dc.
(3 rnds of 24 sts)
Rnd 8: (1 dc in each of next 2 dc, dc2tog) 6 times. (18 sts)
Rnds 9-12: 1 dc in each dc.
(4 rnds of 18 sts)
Rnd 13: (1 dc in the next dc, dc2tog) 6 times. (12 sts)
Fasten off leaving a long tail for sewing.
Stuff the body. Attach the head to the body.

## Legs (make 2)

Using col 1, make a magic ring.
Rnd 1: 6 dc into ring and pull it closed. (6 sts)
Rnd 2: Work 2 dc in each dc. (12 sts)
Rnd 3 (blo): 1 dc in each dc. (12 sts)
Rnd 4: (1 dc in each of next 2 dc, dc2tog) 3 times. (9 sts)
Rnds 5-6: 1 dc in each dc.
(2 rnds of 9 sts)
Fasten off leaving a long tail for sewing.
Stuff the legs.
Cut small round pieces of fabric and sew on the soles.
Attach the legs toward the front of the body.

## Arms (make 2)

Using col 1, make a magic ring.
Rnd 1: 6 dc into ring and pull it closed. (6 sts)
Rnds 2-7: 1 dc in each dc.
(6 rnds of 6 sts)
Fasten off leaving a long tail for sewing.
Using the tail, attach the arms between the head and body.

## Tail

Cut a length of yarn about 40cm long and fold in half. Bring the hook between the stitch spaces at the rear of the body. Grab the yarn and pull up a loop. Ch 5 using both strands. Slip the yarn tail through the last stitch and pull tight. Leave a tail about 1cm long.
Untwist the ends of the yarn to give a tufty look.

## Flower

Using col 2, make a magic ring.
(1 dc, ch 4) 5 times into ring and pull it closed, join with ss in first dc.
Fasten off leaving a long tail for sewing.
Attach the flower to the elephant's head.

# Happy horse

Design a horse that has a playful and floppy head, and is able to stand on his four hooves or sit on his back legs

## Difficulty

★★★★☆

## What you need

- 3.75mm hook (US F/5)
- 1 pair 6mm safety eyes
- Yarn needle
- Fiberfill stuffing
- Scrap of black yarn to embroider mouth and nose
- You will need to use DK weight yarn in your chosen colours. We have used Bernat Handicrafter Cotton:
  Colour 1: Skin (2 balls)
  Colour 2: Mane (1 ball)
  Colour 3: Hooves (1 ball)

## Measurements

22cm tall (when sitting on back legs).

# Pattern

## Head

Using 3.75 mm hook and col 1, make a magic ring.
Rnd 1: 6 dc into ring and pull it closed. (6 sts)
Rnd 2: 2 dc in each dc. (12 sts)
Rnd 3: (1 dc in next dc, 2 dc in next dc) 6 times. (18 sts)
Rnd 4: (1 dc in each of next 2 dc, 2 dc in next dc) 6 times. (24 sts)
Rnds 5-16: 1 dc in each dc.
(12 rnds of 24 sts)

## Assemble the face

Insert 6 mm safety eyes between rnd 12 and rnd 13 of the head and position them 6 sts apart from each other.
Embroider a nose (two nostrils) between rnd 2 and rnd 3 using a yarn needle and black yarn.
Embroider a mouth along 9 sts between rnd 3 and rnd 4.
Stuff the head firmly.
Rnd 17: (1 dc in each of next 2 dc, dc2tog in next 2 dc)
6 times. (18 sts)
Rnd 18: (1 dc in next dc, dc2tog in next 2 dc) 6 times.
(12 sts)
Finish stuffing the head firmly before fastening off.

## Body

Using col 1, make a magic ring.
Rnd 1: 6 dc into ring and pull it closed. (6 sts)
Rnd 2: 2 dc in each dc. (12 sts)
Rnd 3: (1 dc in next dc, 2 dc in next dc) 6 times. (18 sts)
Rnd 4: (1 dc in each of next 2 dc, 2 dc in next dc) 6 times. (24 sts)
Rnd 5: (1 dc in each of next 3 dc, 2 dc in next dc) 6 times. (30 sts)
Rnds 6-21: 1 dc in each dc.
(16 rnds of 30 sts)
Rnd 22: 1 dc in each of next 6 dc, 1 tr in each of next 24 dc. (30 sts)
Rnd 23: 1 dc in each of next 6 dc, (dc2tog in next 2 tr)
12 times. (18 sts)
Rnd 24: 1 dc in each of next 6 dc, 1 tr in each of next 12 dc. (18 sts)
Begin stuffing the body.
Rnd 25: 1 dc in each of next 6 dc, (dc2tog in next 2 tr) 6 times. (12 sts)
Rnd 26: 1 dc in each of next 6 dc, 1 tr in each of next 6 dc. (12 sts)
Rnds 27-36: dc in each st.
(10 rnds of 12 sts)
Finish stuffing the body firmly before fastening off.

## Ears (make 2)

Using col 1, make a magic ring.
Rnd 1: 4 dc into ring and pull it closed. (4 sts)
Rnds 2-4: 1 dc in each dc.
(3 rnds of 4 sts)
Fasten off.

## Legs (make 4)

Using col 3, make a magic ring.
Rnd 1: 6 dc into ring and pull it closed. (6 sts)
Rnd 2: 2 dc in each dc. (12 sts)
Rnd 3 (blo): 1 dc in each dc. (12 sts)
Rnd 4: 1 dc in each dc. (12 sts)
Change to col 1.
Rnd 5 (blo): 1 dc in each dc. (12 sts)
Rnds 6-22: 1 dc in each dc.
(17 rnds of 12 sts) Fasten off.

## Finishing

Stuff the legs.
Join the head to the neck of the body: using the yarn tail from the head, squeeze both pieces flat along top. Work 6 dc straight across through all 4 sts to join as one piece.
Sew the ears to the head between rnd 16 and rnd 17.
Sew 2 of the legs to the bottom of the body between rnd 6 and rnd 9, and position them 2 sts apart.
Sew the other 2 legs to the bottom of the body between rnd 18 and rnd 21, and position them 2 sts apart

## Assemble the mane

Cut 27 15cm strands of col 2.
Fold a strand in half; insert crochet hook into a st on the top of the horse's neck, then insert hook into centre of folded strand; pull the strand up through the st in the neck to form a loop; pull the two ends of the strand through the loop to secure the strand.
Repeat until you have 12 strands on each side of the horse's neck between rnd 24 and rnd 36.
Attach 3 strands using this method to the front of the head to form the forelock and trim the ends.

## Assemble the tail

Cut 20 30cm strands of col 2.
Tie the strands together with another strand in the centre.
Tie this tassel to the end of the horse's body (between rnd 2 and rnd 3) for the tail.

Designed by

## Amy Kember

Amy is a technical writer living in Ottawa, Canada. Her interest in crochet began when she discovered an amigurumi book in a used bookstore. After making a pig, she was instantly hooked. Since 2010, Amy has been designing and selling her own amigurumi patterns on Etsy.
www.etsy.com/shop/AmysGurumis/

# Trio of dinosaurs

Step back to the Jurassic era with these adorable dinosaurs

## Difficulty

★★☆☆☆

## What you need

- 2.75mm hook (US C/2)
- 9mm black safety eyes
- Fiberfill stuffing
- Scissors
- Yarn needle
- Stitch marker (optional)
- You will need an Aran weight yarn in your chosen colours. We have used Rosario 4 Catitano in the following colours:

Colour 1: Green (1 ball)
Colour 2: Dark Green (oddments)
Colour 3: Grey (oddments)

## Measurements

20cm head to tail.

Designed by
**Mevlinn Gusick**

Mevlinn is a college graduate with a BFA in Fine Arts Painting. Her interest in knitting and crochet began when her aunt suggested she try knitting. It peaked her curiosity and here she is today, crocheting amigurumi whenever she gets the chance and giving them to those she loves.
www.mevvsan.com

## Stegosaurus

### body and head

Using col 1, make a magic ring.
Rnd 1: 7 dc in magic ring. (7 sts)
Rnd 2: 2 dc in each st around. (14 sts)
Rnd 3: (2 dc in next st, 1 dc next st) 7 times. (21 sts)
Rnd 4: (2 dc in next st, 1 dc in next 2 sts) 7 times. (28 sts)
Rnd 5: (2 dc in next st, 1 dc in next 3 sts) 7 times. (35 sts)
Rnd 6: 1 dc in each st around. (35 sts)
Rnd 7: (2 dc in next st, 1 dc in next 4 sts) 7 times. (42 sts)
Rnd 8: 1 dc in each st around. (42 sts)
Rnd 9: 2 dc in next st, 1 dc in next st, 2 dc in next st, 1 dc in next 39 sts. (44 sts)

Note: Rnd 9 is the start of a side specific increase made to create the 'hump' of the Stegosaurus's back. Keep this in mind later when placing the eyes.

Rnd 10: 1 dc in each st around. (44 sts)
Rnd 11: 2 dc in next st, 1 dc in next st, 2 dc in next st, 1 dc in next 41 sts. (46 sts)
Rnd 12-13: 1 dc in each st around. (2 rnds of 46 sts)
Rnd 14: dc2tog, 1 dc in next st, dc2tog, 1 dc in next 41 sts. (44 sts)
Rnd 15: 1 dc in each st around. (44 sts)
Rnd 16: dc2tog, 1 dc in next st, dc2tog, 1 dc in next 39 sts. (42 sts)
Rnd 17: 1 dc in each st around. (42 sts)
Rnd 18: (dc2tog, 1 dc in next 5 sts) 6 times. (36 sts)
Rnd 19: 1 dc in each st around. (36 sts)
Start stuffing and continue stuffing as you go.
Rnd 20: (dc2tog, 1 dc in next 4 sts) 6 times. (30 sts)
Rnd 21: 1 dc in each st around. (30 sts)
Rnd 22: (dc2tog, 1 dc in next 3 sts) 6 times. (24 sts)
Rnd 23: 1 dc in each st around. (24 sts)
Rnd 24: (dc2tog, 1 dc in next 2 sts) 6 times. (18 sts)
Rnd 25-27: 1 dc in each st around. (3 rnds of 18 sts)
Fix safety eyes between rnds 25-27 with 8 sts between each eye.
Rnd 28: (dc2tog, 1 dc in next 7 sts) twice. (16 sts)
Rnd 29: (dc2tog, 1 dc in next 2 sts) 4 times. (12 sts)
Rnd 30: (dc2tog) 6 times. (6 sts)
Fasten off and sing a wool needle, weave the yarn tail through the front ring of each remaining st and pull to close.

### Tail

Using col 1, make a magic ring.
Rnd 1: 4 dc in magic ring. (4 sts)
Rnd 2: 1 dc in each st around. (4 sts)
Rnd 3: 2 dc in next st, 1 dc in each remaining st to end. (5 sts)
Rnds 4-22: Rep rnd 3. (24 sts after rnd 22)
Fasten off, leaving a tail for sewing. Stuff the tail and sew it onto the body.

Note: When sewing the tail to the body, place the body on a table and pin the tail in place. You want the tail to be attached to the body but touching the table in a completely horizontal position. If you try and sew the tail at an angle to the body you might find that the tail stops the legs from resting on the ground when you sew them on later.

### Front legs (make 2)

Using col 1, make a magic ring.
Rnd 1: 6 dc in magic ring. (6 sts)
Rnd 2: 2 dc in each st around. (12 sts)
Rnd 3 (blo): 1 dc in each st around. (12 sts)
Rnds 4-8: 1 dc in each st around. (5 rnds of 12 sts)
Fasten off, leaving a long tail for sewing.

## Back legs (make 2)

Using col 1, make a magic ring.
Rnds 1-8: As given for Front Legs. (12 sts)
Rnds 9-10: 1 dc in each st around. (2 rnds of 12 sts)
Fasten off, leaving a long tail for sewing.

## Sewing on the legs

First stuff each leg firmly at the bottom, and less firmly at the top so that you can pinch the opening shut, folding it in half. Now find a spot on the side of the dinosaur where you want to attach the leg. Hold the body while you're doing this and position it above a table. You want the legs to give the body enough lift so that the stomach won't touch the table.

Thread your yarn and sew only the top half of the leg in place. Then sew one row down and continue sewing the rest of the leg in place. It should be very thin at the joint and may be awkward. Instead of fastening off, thread the yarn to the underside of the leg and begin sewing the leg to the body, one st at a time. Go down the leg about 3-5 sts until you see the bowed leg finally tighten up and line up straight with the side of the body. When you are happy with the leg fasten off, and weave the yarn end into the body.

Note: The stegosaurus has longer hind legs than front, so allow for this when attaching them. Always keep in mind how you want your dinosaur's finished position to be when attaching their legs.

## Small spike (make 6)

Using col 2, make a magic ring.
Rnd 1: 5 dc in magic ring. (5 sts)
Rnd 2: 2 dc in each st around. (10 sts)
Rnd 3: (dc2tog) 5 times. (5 sts)
Fasten off, leaving a long tail for sewing. Do not stuff the spikes.

## Medium spike (make 4)

Using col 2, make a magic ring.
Rnd 1: 5 dc in magic ring. (5 sts)
Rnd 2: 2 dc in each st around. (10 sts)
Rnd 3: (2 dc in next st, 1 dc in next 4 sts) twice. (12 sts)
Rnd 4: (dc2tog, 1 dc in next 4 sts) twice. (10 sts)
Rnd 5: (dc2tog) 5 times. (5 sts)
Fasten off, leaving a long tail for sewing. Do not stuff the spikes.

## Large spike (make 2)

Using col 2, make a magic ring.
Rnd 1: 5 dc in magic ring. (5 sts)
Rnd 2: 2 dc in each st around. (10 sts)
Rnd 3: (2 dc in next st, 1 dc in next st) 5 times. (15 sts)
Rnd 4: 1 dc in each st around. (15 sts)
Rnd 5: (dc2tog, 1 dc in next st) 5 times. (10 sts)
Rnd 6: (dc2tog) 5 times. (5 sts)
Fasten off, leaving a long tail for sewing. Do not stuff the spikes.

## Finishing

Sew the spikes evenly spaced down the body and tail of the Stegosaurus. Starting at the head, you will have two rows of spikes side by side in the following order, working from front to back: Small/Medium/Large/Medium/Small/Small.

The two rows maintain a little over a finger's width apart but narrow more as they reach the tail and head.

## Toenails

Using col 3, cut a length of yarn about as long as your arm and attach it to the edge of the foot, ch 3, 1 dc back into the same st (one toenail made). *Pull the yarn through as if you were fastening off, but instead

thread a needle and move the yarn two sts to the left for the next toenail, ch 3, 1 dc back into the same st; rep from * once more to make the third and final toenail.
Fasten off and weave in all yarn ends.

## Tail spikes (make 4)

Using col 3, make a magic ring.
Rnd 1: 4 dc in magic ring. (4 sts)
Rnd 2: 2 dc in next st, 1 dc in each remaining st. (5 sts)
Rnd 3: 1 dc in each st around. (5 sts)
Rnd 4: 2 dc in next st, 1 dc in each remaining st. (6 sts)
Rnd 5: 1 dc in each st around. (6 sts)
Fasten off, leaving a long tail for sewing. Do not stuff the spikes. Sew the spikes to the tip of the dinosaur's tail, two on each side.

## Difficulty

★ ★ ★ ☆ ☆

## What you need

- 2.75 mm (US C/2)
- 12 mm black safety eyes
- Fiberfill stuffing
- Scissors
- Yarn needle
- Stitch marker (optional)
- You will need Aran weight yarn in your chosen colours. We have used Rosario 4 Catitano in:
  Colour 1: Orange (1 ball)
  Colour 2: Light yellow (oddments):

## Measurements

25cm head to tail.

# T-Rex

## Body

Using col 1, make a magic ring.
Rnd 1: 6 dc in magic ring. (6 sts)
Rnd 2: 2 dc in each st around. (12 sts)
Rnd 3: (2 dc in next st, 1 dc in next st) 6 times. (18 sts)
Rnd 4: (2 dc in next st, 1 dc in next 2 sts) 6 times. (24 sts)
Rnd 5: (2 dc in next st, 1 dc in next 3 sts) 6 times. (30 sts)
Rnd 6: (2 dc in next st, 1 dc in next 4 sts) 6 times. (36 sts)
Rnd 7: 1 dc in each st around. (36 sts)
Rnd 8: (2 dc in next st, 1 dc in next 5 sts) 6 times. (42 sts)
Rnds 9-10: 1 dc in each st around. (2 rnds of 42 sts)
Rnd 11: dc2tog, 1 dc in each remaining st to end. (41 sts)
Rnds 12-14: As rnd 11. (38 sts after rnd 14)
Stuff with toy fi lling and continue stuffi ng as you go.
Rnd 15: dc2tog, 1 dc in next 33 sts, dc2tog, 1 dc in last st. (36 sts)
Rnd 16: dc2tog, 1 dc in next 31 sts, dc2tog, 1 dc in last st. (34 sts)
Rnd 17: dc2tog, 1 dc in next 29 sts, dc2tog, 1 dc in last st. (32 sts)
Rnd 18: dc2tog, 1 dc in next 27 sts, dc2tog, 1 dc in last st. (30 sts)
Rnd 19: dc2tog, 1 dc in next 25 sts, dc2tog, 1 dc in last st. (28 sts)
Rnd 20: dc2tog, 1 dc in next 23 sts, dc2tog, 1 dc in last st. (26 sts)
Rnd 21: dc2tog, 1 dc in each remaining st to end. (25 sts)
Rnds 22-26: As rnd 21. (20 sts after rnd 26)
Fasten off, leaving a long tail for sewing.

## Head

Using col 1, make a magic ring.
Rnd 1: 6 dc in magic ring. (6 sts)
Rnd 2: 2 dc in each st around. (12 sts)
Rnd 3: (2 dc in next st, 1 dc in next st) 6 times. (18 sts)
Rnd 4: (2 dc in next st, 1 dc in next 2 sts) 6 times. (24 sts)
Rnd 5: (2 dc in next st, 1 dc in next 3 sts) 6 times. (30 sts)
Rnd 6: (2 dc in next st, 1 dc in next 4 sts) 6 times. (36 sts)
Rnds 7-15: 1 dc in each st around. (9 rnds of 36 sts)
Rnd 16: (dc2tog, 1 dc in next 4 sts) 6 times. (30 sts)
Rnd 17: (dc2tog, 1 dc in next 3 sts) 6 times. (24 sts)
Fix the safety eyes 11 rows down from the magic ring with 13 sts between each eye. Start stuffing and continue stuffing as you go.
Rnd 18: (dc2tog, 1 dc in next 2 sts) 6 times. (18 sts)
Rnd 19: (dc2tog, 1 dc in next st) 6 times. (12 sts)
Rnd 20: (dc2tog) 6 times. (6 sts)
Fasten off, leaving a tail for sewing. Using a yarn needle, weave the yarn tail through the front ring of each remaining st and pull it tight to close. Using the tail, sew the head to the body. (The back of the neck should be sewn onto the head approx 6 rnds away from the head's magic ring.)

## Tail

Using col 1, make a magic ring.
Rnd 1: 4 dc in magic ring. (4 sts)
Rnd 2: 1 dc in each st around. (4 sts)
Rnd 3: 2 dc in next st, 1 dc in each remaining st. (5 sts)
Rnds 4-25: Rep rnd 3. (27 sts after rnd 25)
Fasten off, leaving a long tail for sewing. Stuff the tail with fiberfill and sew it to the body as follows: Place the body on a table in an upright position and pin the tail in place first. If you try to sew the tail on at an angle to the body, you might find that it stops the legs from resting on the ground when you sew them on later.

## Legs (make 2)

Using col 1, make a magic ring.
Rnd 1: 6 dc in magic ring (6 sts)
Rnd 2: 2 dc in each st around. (12 sts)
Rnd3 (blo): 1 dc in each st around. (12 sts)
Rnds 4-9: 1 dc in each st around. (6 rnds of 12 sts)
Fasten off, leaving a long tail for sewing.

## Arms (make 2)

Using col 1, make a magic ring.
Rnd 1: 4 dc in magic ring. (4 sts)
Rnds 2-7: 1 dc in each st around. (6 rnds of 4 sts)
Fasten off, leaving a long tail for sewing.

## Fingers (make 2)

Using col 1, make a magic ring.
Rnd 1: 4 dc in magic ring. (4 sts)
Rnds 2-3: 1 dc in each st around. (2 rnds of 4 sts)
Fasten off, leaving a long tail for sewing. When both the arms and fingers are complete, sew the finger to the arm so that the end of the arm and the finger are both of equal length. Sew the arms to the body approx 7-8 rows below the point where the head attaches to the body.

## Toenails

Using col 2, cut a length of yarn about as long as your arm and attach it to the edge of the foot, ch 3, 1 dc back into the same st (one toenail made). *Pull the yarn through two sts to the left for the next toenail, ch 3, 1 dc back into the same st; rep from * once more to make the final toenail.
Fasten off and weave in ends.

## Nail tips

Using col 2, cut a short piece of yarn and pull the yarn through a st at the tip of a finger, ch 1, move the hook to a st to the left of the finger, 1 dc, ch 1, pull the yarn through and fasten off. Weave in the yarn ends gently to avoid distorting the ch 1 tip to the nail you just made.

## Finishing

First stuff each leg firmly at the bottom, and less firmly at the top so that you can pinch the opening shut, folding it in half. Now find a spot on the side of the dinosaur where you want to attach the leg. Hold the body above a table as far as you want it to stand when all the legs are sewn on. Go down the leg about 3-5 sts until you see the bowed leg finally tighten and line up straight with the side of the body.
Fasten off and weave in the yarn end.

Note: To keep all legs even you need to attach each leg at the exact same row on the body.

## Difficulty

★★★☆☆

## What you need

- 2.75 mm (US C/2)
- 12 mm black safety eyes
- Fiberfill stuffing
- Scissors
- Yarn needle
- Stitch marker (optional)
- In this pattern we have used Rosario 4 Catitano. You will need an aran weight yarn in the following colours:
  Colour 1: Beige (1 ball)
  Colour 2: Brown (oddments)
  Colour 3: White (oddments)

## Measurements

25cm head to tail.

# Triceratops

## Body

Using col 1, make a magic ring.
Rnd 1: 7 dc in magic ring. (7 sts)
Rnd 2: 2 dc in each st around. (14 sts)
Rnd 3: (2 dc in next st, 1 dc next st) 7 times. (21 sts)
Rnd 4: (2 dc in next st, 1 dc in next 2 sts) 7 times. (28 sts)
Rnd 5: (2 dc in next st, 1 dc in next 3 sts) 7 times. (35 sts)
Rnd 6: 1 dc in each st around. (35 sts)
Rnd 7: (2 dc in next st, 1 dc in next 4 sts) 7 times. (42 sts)
Rnds 8-13: 1 dc in each st around. (6 rnds of 42 sts)
Rnd 14: (dc2tog, 1 dc in next 5 sts) 6 times. (36 sts)
Rnd 15: 1 dc in each st around. (36 sts)
Start stuffing and continue stuffing as you go.
Rnd 16: (dc2tog, 1 dc in next 7 sts) 4 times. (32 sts)
Rnd 17: 1 dc in each st around. (32 sts)
Rnd 18: (dc2tog, 1 dc in next 6 sts) 4 times. (28 sts)
Rnds 19-20: 1 dc in each st around. (2 rnds of 28 sts)
Fasten off, leaving a tail for sewing.

## Head

Using col 1, make a magic ring.
Rnd 1: 6 dc in magic ring. (6 sts)
Rnd 2: 2 dc in each st around. (12 sts)
Rnd 3: 1 dc in each st around. (12 sts)
Rnd 4: (2 dc in next st, 1 dc in next st) 6 times. (18 sts)
Rnd 5: 1 dc in each st around. (18 sts)
Rnd 6: (2 dc in next st, 1 dc in next 2 sts) 6 times. (24 sts)
Rnd 7: (2 dc in next st, 1 dc in next 3 sts) 6 times. (30 sts)
Rnd 8: (2 dc in next st, 1 dc in next 4 sts) 6 times. (36 sts)
Rnds 9-11: 1 dc in each st around. (3 rnds of 36 sts)
Rnd 12: 1 dcblo in next 18 sts (this will help you to identify where to crochet the head crest later), 1 dc in each remaining st (working through both rings). (36 sts)
Rnd 13: (dc2tog, 1 dc in next 4 sts) 6 times. (30 sts)

Fix the safety eyes 7 rows down from magic ring with 14 sts between each eye.
Start stuffing and continue stuffing as you go.

Rnd 14: (dc2tog, 1 dc in next 3 sts) 6 times. (24 sts)
Rnd 15: (dc2tog, 1 dc in next 2 sts) 6 times (18 sts)
Rnd 16: (dc2tog, 1 dc in next st) 6 times. (12 sts)
Rnd 17: (dc2tog) 6 times. (6 sts)
Fasten off, leaving a tail for sewing. Weave the yarn tail through the front ring of each remaining st and pull it tight to close.

## Head crest

Using col 1, with the front of the triceratops's head facing you, attach yarn with a sl st to the far right unworked ring from rnd 12 of the head.
Row 1: ch 3 (counts as 1 tr), tr in the same ring at base of ch 3, 1 tr in next 7 rings, 2 tr in next 2 rings, 1 tr in next 7 rings, 2 tr in last ring, turn. (22 sts)
Row 2: ch 2, (counts as 1 htr), 1 htr in same st at base of ch 2, 1 tr in next 9 sts, 2 tr in next 2 sts, 1 tr in next 9 sts, 2 htr in last st, turn. (26 sts)
Row 3: ch 2, 1 htr in same st at base of ch 2, 1 tr in next 11 sts, 2 tr in next 2 sts, 1 tr in next 11 sts, 2 htr in last st, turn. (30 sts)
Change to col 2.
Row 4: *1 dc in next 2 sts, (1 htr, ch 2, 1 htr) in next st; rep from * to end.
Fasten off, weave in ends.

## Head horns (make 2)

Using col 3, make a magic ring.
Rnd 1: 4 dc in magic ring. (4 sts)
Rnd 2: 1 dc in each st around. (4 sts)
Rnd 3: 2 dc in next st, 1 dc in next 3 sts. (5 sts)
Rnd 4: 2 dc in next st, 1 dc in next 4 sts. (6 sts)
Rnd 5: 2 dc in next st, 1 dc in next 5 sts. (7 sts)
Rnd 6: 2 dc in next st, 1 dc in next 6 sts. (8 sts)
Fasten off, leaving a long tail. Lightly stuff if needed and sew a horn above each eye.

## Nose horn

Using col 3, make a magic ring.
Rnd 1: 4 dc in magic ring. (4 sts)
Rnd 2: 1 dc in each st around. (4 sts)
Rnd 3: 2 dc in next st, 1 dc in next 3 sts. (5 sts)
Rnd 4: 2 dc in next st, 1 dc in next 4 sts. (6 sts)
Rnd 5: 2 dc in next st, 1 dc in next 5 sts. (7 sts)
Fasten off, leaving a tail for sewing. Lightly stuff if needed and sew this horn to the tip of the nose.

Using the tail end of yarn from the body, sew the head to the body.

## Tail

Using col 1, make a magic ring.
Rnd 1: 4 dc in magic ring. (4 sts)
Rnd 2: 1 dc in each st around. (4 sts)
Rnd 3: 2 dc in next st, 1 dc in each remaining st to end. (5 sts)
Rnds 4-21: As rnd 3. (23 sts after rnd 21)
Fasten off, leaving a long tail for sewing.
Stuff the tail with toy filling and sew it onto the body as follows: Place the body onto a table and pin the tail in place first. You want the tail to be attached to the body and be completely horizontal with the table. If you try to sew the tail on at an angle to the body

you might find that the tail stops the legs from resting on the ground when you later sew them on.

## Front legs (make 2)

Using col 1, make a magic ring.
Rnd 1: 6 dc in magic ring. (6 sts)
Rnd 2: 2 dc in each st around. (12 sts)
Rnd 3 (blo): 1 dc in each st around. (12 sts)
Rnds 4-9: 1 dc in each st around. (6 rnds of 12 sts)
Fasten off, leaving a long tail for sewing.

## Back legs (make 2)

Using col 1, make a magic ring.
Rnds 1-9: As given for Front Legs. (12 sts)
Rnd 10: 1 dc in each st around. (12 sts)
Fasten off, leaving a long tail for sewing.

## Sewing on the legs

Hold the body while you're doing this and position it above a table as far as you want it to stand when all the legs are sewn on. You want the legs to give the body enough lift off the table so that the stomach won't touch the table when it is completely assembled.
First stuff each leg firmly at the bottom, and less firmly at the top so that you can pinch the opening shut, folding it in half. Now find a spot on the side of the dinosaur where you want to attach the leg.
Thread your yarn and sew only the top half of the leg in place. Then sew one row down and continue sewing the rest of the leg in place into this row. It should be very thin at the joint and may be awkward. Instead of fastening off, thread the yarn to the underside of the leg and begin sewing the leg to the body, one st at a time. Go down the leg about 3-5 sts until you see the bowed leg finally tighten and line up straight with the side of the body. When you are happy with the leg, fasten off and weave the yarn end into the body.

Note: The triceratops has longer hind legs, and this helps to push its face closer to the ground, so make sure you attach the legs to different rows to make it even. Always keep in mind how you want your dinosaur's finished position to be when attaching their legs.

## Toenails

Using col 2, cut a length of yarn about as long as your arm, and attach it to the edge of the foot, ch 4, 1 tr back into the same st (one toenail made). *Pull the yarn through as if you were fastening off, but instead thread a needle and move the yarn two sts to the left for the next toenail, ch 4, 1 tr back into the same st; rep from * once more to make the third and final toenail.
Fasten off, weave in all ends.